W9-CKH-523

# The World of Seashells

## A Fully Illustrated Guide to These Fascinating Gifts From the Ocean

# The World of Seashells

## A Fully Illustrated Guide to These Fascinating Gifts From the Ocean

Patrick Hook

GRAMERCY BOOKS

NEW YORK

First published in 1998 by PRC Publishing Ltd,
Kiln House, 210 New Kings Road, London SW6 4NZ
© 1998 by Random House Value Publishing, Inc.
All rights reserved under International and Pan-American Copyright Conventions
No Part of this book may be reproduced or transmitted in any
form or by any means electronic or mechanical including
photocopying, recording, or by any information storage and
retrieval system, without permission in writing from the publisher.

This edition is published by Gramercy Books,®
a division of Random House Value Publishing, Inc.,
201 East 50th Street, New York, New York, 10022.

Gramercy Books® and design are registered trademarks of
Random House Value Publishing, Inc.
Random House
New York • Toronto • London • Sydney • Auckland
http://www.randomhouse.com/

Printed and bound in China
A CIP catalogue record for this book is available from the Library of Congress.

ISBN 0-517-16132-X

8 7 6 5 4 3 2 1

# Glossary

**Aberrant:** When an individual is markedly different from others of its species.

**Adductor muscles:** Found in bivalves — they are The muscles which close the two valves tightly.

**Biota:** Expression used to describe the flora and fauna of a habitat.

**Byssus:** The threads bivalves use to attach themselves to the substrate (rocks, jetties, etc.).

**Callosity or Callus:** A localized area of thickening of the shell.

**Cardinal:** The central hinge tooth found in bivalves.

**Conchology:** The study of shells; today it means the study of the shell only, that is, not the living organism inside.

**Descriptor:** Person who first described the species for science, and the date when published.

**Endemic:** When a species is native to or confined to a certain area.

**Exhalent siphon:** The tubular extension of bivalves through which they circulate water from the mantle cavity.

**Inhalant siphon:** The more ventral tubular extension of bivalves through which water is sucked into the mantle cavity — from this the mollusk filters out its nutritional supply. Some gastropods also have an inhalant siphon.

**Ligament:** The "spring" which opens the two halves of bivalves. The adductor muscles work against it when the mollusk pulls the halves shut. This why dead bivalves always have their valves open.

**Mollusk (UK: Mollusc):** derives from the Latin *mollis*, which means "soft". It encompasses any invertebrate of the phylum Mollusca; often these mollusks have shells — but not always.

**Niche:** The position that an organism takes up within an particular ecosystem, e.g. limpets on rocks.

**Operculum:** The trapdoor that gastropods use to seal themselves against the outside world, usually a horny or calcareous disc attached to the foot.

**Polymorphism:** This means that a species has several different forms.

**Population:** The number of individuals of a given species in a certain habitat or geographical area.

**Radula:** The "rasping tongue" of most mollusks. When seen under a microscope, it is a bit like a conveyor belt with cutting teeth inserted into it.

**Siphonal/anterior canal:** The groove through which the inhalant siphon passes.

# Contents

# Introduction

Shells have fascinated mankind ever since civilization began. They have been represented in art through paintings and sculptures, in finance as currency, and in battle as heraldic symbols. In fact, my own family coat of arms has four "escallopes invert" — that is, upside-down scallop shells, as the major elements of its design.

One of the attractions of shell collecting is that it is within the reach of everyone — it is true that the rarer specimens can fetch vast sums of money, but at the other end of the spectrum, they are free for the taking. Very often the fascination with shells starts at an early age with slow walks along the beach under the patient supervision of family members. If these early forays were anything like mine, the wonderful fruits of this collection would soon end up on the flower-bed — my father would use them as extra calcium for his beloved plants!

Over the years, there have been a few people who have made themselves famous by collecting and/or writing about shells — some of the collections put together were spectacular, and some of the books on the subject have been works of art in their own right.

Every single species of shell also has its place in nature, along with all the complex interactions that this implies. Some are predators, and all are prey. Some are abundant, while others are on the edge of extinction. Many are edible, but others are highly poisonous. While most are entirely harmless to man, there are others that are capable of inflicting fatal wounds if handled carelessly, or trodden on by the unwary.

Some people will find their almost endless variety of shapes and colors to be enough to sustain a life-long fascination, but for many others, the driving rationale is to study their biology — that is, how shells coexist with their environment.

Much of the scientific research into shell species is focused on those with commercial significance, such as abalones, mussels and oysters. Sometimes the financial return is from turning the meat of the mollusk into food, while in others it is for the production of pearls, or the production of "artifacts", such as jewelry, or tourist gifts.

We have found and scientifically described over 100,000 different species of shells — but this is estimated to be only half of them. This isn't surprising: our planet's surface is four-fifths water, and it we know more about the surface of the moon than we do about the bottom of our seas and oceans!

This book can only scratch the surface of the subject, but I hope that it will serve as a starting point for those newly arrived at the subject, and thought-provoking for the existing enthusiast.

*Patrick Hook*

# Shells: what they are and how they are constructed

**Right: This is an excellent illustration of how a nautilus shell is constructed. The living mollusc controls its buoyancy by pumping water in and out of these chambers.**

**Below: Sand dollars are often found washed up on beaches and are commonly mistaken for seashells by newcomers to the shoreline. They are, in fact, sea urchins, which are members of the *echinodermata* and therefore far removed from the *mollusca*.**

What constitutes a "shell"? Today there are clear guidelines: if it's not in the phylum mollusca, it's not a shell! It wasn't this straightforward in the past. In the 18th century, shells were considered to include any animal that had a rigid exterior covering, for example crabs, lobsters, and sea urchins, all of which are in different categories today (crabs and lobsters are crustaceans; sea urchins are echinoderms). The modern classification was initiated by Baron Georges Cuvier who grouped mollusks (the word "mollusk" derives from the Latin *mollis*, meaning soft) together in much the way they are now, except that he included the barnacles and brachiopods — these are now placed in the crustacea and brachiopoda.

Not all mollusk species possess a shell: take the slug — a mollusk, and yet quite obviously shell-less. The slug highlights another distinction: not all mollusks come from the sea. Many live on land or in fresh water. "Shellfish" is also a misnomer: it's not a scientific word, but one used to cover seafood that has some form of hard outer covering, and hence covers not only mollusks but also shrimps, prawns, crabs, lobsters, etc.

Why do some mollusks grow shells in the first place? Mostly for protection against predators. The shell protects the mollusk for long enough for it to be able to breed, but at a metabolic construction cost low enough not to reduce its breeding success. There's a trade-off: the shell must be strong enough to protect the tasty morsel inside from predators and still be practical to build — and the fact that shells have been around for so many millions of years tells us that this has been achieved with a great deal of success. They are bio-engineered with a very clever blend of design and materials, and — as with so much in nature — there are many superb optimizations of form and function in shell structures.

In the marine environment most predators attack their prey using force — for example the trigger fish uses powerful jaws to crunch its way through coral or crustacea. Shells consist of calcium carbonate crystals embedded in a matrix of protein. The crystals are of aragonite — a mineral which is also found naturally in rock. The inner surfaces of most shells is made of "nacre", but in some species it is used to create the entire thickness of the shell — including the Pearly Nautilus and the Pearl Oyster. Each crystal of aragonite is in the shape of a small platelet, measuring 5 x 5 x 0.5 microns; these are laid down in layers, glued together with special proteins. The clever part is that the shell allows very small cracks to occur when it is attacked, but it dissipates them so effectively that they don't combine to produce an actual breakage. It is, therefore, extremely difficult for a predator to form a crack without exerting far more force than would be reasonable.

The limiting factor of nacre strength is the protein that glues the platelets together: they fail when pulled apart, not by snapping. Nacre produces a slow and steady failure, requiring a lot of energy to get through, instead of a sudden collapse. Few predators expend enough energy to make the shell give way, allowing the mollusk to live for another day, and repair the damage. The fact that nacre is built up of crystals and protein makes it a composite material — just as carbon fibre, kevlar and glass fibre are combined with resins to produce tough, durable structures, such as boats, aircraft and racing cars.

Shells are also constructed so that their maximum strength is in the direction of expected attack from a predator — in other words, from outside. The energy required to produce a crack from outside is ten times that required to produce one along the length of the shell, thus saving the mollusk from expending its resources constructing needless material strength, and yet another example of the way that human engineers can learn lessons from nature!

# Shell classification: how they are named

One of the problems with the classification of any plant or animal order is that it doesn't stay the same for very long — the taxonomists are forever arguing about the relevance of certain morphological features, whether a particular tubercle is more significant than a given bristle, and so on. There is no single system that everyone agrees will be universal. The truth is that every system is an entirely artificial ordering — one that we, as humans, have decided to impose on the natural world for our own convenience. In other words, whatever I say here, some people will disagree with it, and the odds are it will be out of date before I get to the end of the paragraph anyway!

A lot of shells have an English, or common, name, and all those that we have found have one in Latin — the scientific name; this latter is derived from the "binomial" system which was first used by Carl Linnaeus (properly written Carl Von Linné) in 1753, in his book *Species Plantarum*. This was the starting point for scientific nomenclature for botanists, and the same happened for zoologists when Linnaeus published his tenth edition of *Systema Naturae* in 1758. What made him unique amongst scientists of his time was that he was a very systematic worker. Can you imagine the mess we'd be in today if Linnaeus had tried to impose a naming system on over a million different animal species without it being rigorous and methodical?

The Latin name has at least two parts, and may well have "extra" names tacked on the end. Sometimes they translate into meaningful phrases, especially those named back in Linnaeus's time. For instance, the "Elongate Tusk," named in 1842, is known scientifically as *Dentalium longitrorsum*, which translates as "Long Tooth" — rather unsurprisingly as it looks just like one!

When the species in question has various subspecies, an addition is

**Far Right: Some seashells have common names that don't make any obvious sense. Others, such as this blood tooth, need no explanation.**

**Right: The Black-Spotted Triton was described for science by Linnaeus in 1758, so these details are added to the end of its scientific name thus: *Cymatium lotorium*, Linnaeus 1758. (See page 123.)**

made to the name; for instance, when the "Rock Shell," Latin name *Thais haemostoma*, is considered, the subspecies from Florida has the word *floridana* added, so it becomes *Thais haemostoma floridana*. Notice also, that the first letter of the Latin name is spelt with a capital (this is the "generic" name), whereas the first letter of the second (this is the "specific" name) and any others are in lower case.

You will often also see a name and, possibly, a date at the end of the Latin name, such as "Conrad, 1837." This identifies who first described the species for science, and the date when the description was published. However, if this name and date are placed in parentheses, it means that the species has been moved from the genus where it was first put into another one. This may sound a bit much, but it's scientific convention — it also helps to clarify the situation if someone else uses the same Latin name for a different species.

One of the other confusing aspects of naming any plant or animal is that, as we discover more and more about which species are related to which, we have to re-classify them — that is, we have to take them out of the place where we formerly thought they belonged in the family tree of life, and put them in what we hope is the right place. This means that we have to change their Latin name. To make matters even more confusing, a single species may have many different common names, even in the same country. For instance the shell known as the "Lance Auger" in some countries is known as the "Marlinspike" in others.

# The classes of the phylum mollusca

The phylum mollusca contains some real surprises if we expect it to contain "just" shells, for it also includes the cephalopods — so the octopus and the squid are in this varied group. It also covers several more familiar classes, including the bivalves (scallops and clams), the gastropods (slugs and snails), scaphopods (tusk shells), and the polyplacophorans (chitons). There are two others which are much less well known; these are the aplacophorans (solenogasters), and the monoplacophorans.

### Class Aplacophora
The aplacophorans are worm-like creatures that don't have shells in much the same way that slugs don't, so they are less well known to shell-collectors than more conventional classes. They are marine animals that vary tremendously in size: some are only 0.04in long (1mm), whereas others grow up to a foot in length (300mm). The 250 or so species divide into two types — those that are predators, and those that feed on detritus.

**The nautilus shell has buoyancy chambers and can float a long way even after the mollusk which created it has died. Because of this, when you find a nautilus it is impossible to know where it came from.**

### Class Monoplacophora
Until the 1950s, when the first living species was found, it was thought that the monoplacophorans had been extinct for between 50 and 370 million years, as they were only known from the fossil record. Since then more recent discoveries have brought the current total to about 12 known species. Rarely seen by shell-collectors as they live in deep water — sometimes very deep water indeed, ranging from between 600ft (183m) and 20,000ft (6,100m) in depth — they vary in size from about 0.1in (2.5mm) up to about 1.5in (38mm); they are very simple mollusks with limpet-like shells that feed on things like algae.

### Class Polyplacophora — Chitons
The polyplacophorans are sometimes called the "coat-of-mail" shells, as they usually have eight plates that overlap like medieval armor. These are attached to each other with strong fibres, producing a tough and durable defence against most predators. The 800 or so members of the class are entirely marine; most are shallow water species, but some extend into the abyssal depths. They are grazers on various marine growths, in much the same manner as the limpets with which they often share their habitat.

### Class Scaphopoda — Tusk shells
The Tusk shells are uncommon marine animals that have tubular shells which bear more than a passing resemblance to the tusks of, for example, an elephant. The most obvious difference (apart from size!) is that the shells are open at both ends. There are about 350 species, ranging in size from 6in (150mm) down to about a 0.1in (2.5mm). Their preferred habitats tend to be where there is soft sand or mud to bury themselves.

**Below: These three W.D. & H.O. Wills cigarette cards are part of a series on the seashore. They show a cluster of edible mussels, acorn barnacles on a mussel shell, and the egg-case of a dogfish which should not be mistaken for a mollusk.**

*Class Cephalopoda — Octopus, Squid, etc.*

The cephalopods are one of the most fascinating groups of animals to occur anywhere; the group includes the nautilus, the octopus, the squid, the argonauts, and the cuttlefish. Some of Class Cephalopoda possess amazing eyesight, which makes sense when you consider their advanced — mainly visual — communication mechanisms. Some squid, for example, pass complicated messages via skin coloration. This is achieved by having "chromatophoric" pigmentation, which means that they can change color and some can do this at a tremendous speed.

It has been observed that individuals are able to "say" different things with each side of their body; for example, if a male has other males to his right, but a female to his left, and wants a personal "conversation" with her, he can maintain a neutral message to his contemporaries, but present a quite different, and presumably highly personal, series of signals to the female.

Many of the Cephalopods are intelligent, especially for invertebrates. Some of them are quite small, such as the male argonaut at about 0.5in (13mm), right up to the giant squid, which may exceed 65ft (20m). No-one is quite sure how big they get, with the stories of seafarers usually being considered to be exaggerated. There are records of whales being marked by some creature — almost certainly the giant squid and from the size of the scars left by the suckers, they were very large indeed. They are rumors that even submarines have been attacked by squid which presumably mistook them for whales!

The difficulty with finding out much about giant squid is that they live in very deep waters, with only occasional sightings at or near the surface. They are hunted by sperm whales, which make deep dives to seek them out. One ambitious project currently underway is an attempt to film the giant squid by attaching film cameras to whales using temporary harnesses. The idea is to get film when the whale tracks down and eats this legendary creature — although it appears from the marks on some whales that this is anything but a one-sided event.

Squid are not the only members of this group that grow to enormous size. One of the many stories brought back from tropical explorations was that of Evelyn Cheesman, who was a Fellow of the Royal Entomological Society. She wrote about an insect hunting trip to what was then called "Dutch New Guinea" (since renamed "Papua New Guinea") in 1937-39, in her book *Camping Adventures In New Guinea*. At one point in her trip, she tells us, she decided to make a painting of Fak-fak Bay from Mount Nok. She says that she was four miles from the bay, and that, "The sea was perfectly calm and very blue, but in the bay was one white patch on the water."

After much discussion with her native guides, she found out that it was a giant octopus, something they were quite used to seeing. The natives told her that there were two of them that lived in different bays, and each had been given local names. They lived in deep water, but occasionally came to the surface, where they would grab any canoes that were unfortunate enough to be within reach. If the occupants were lucky, the octopus would be happy with the contents of the fish baskets left behind, and they would have time to swim for the shore. However, one woman was too keen to save her fish, and got caught "by those monstrous arms and was never seen again."

The cephalopods are characterized by having tentacles around the head, and by having a form of "jet propulsion" provided via a sort of nozzle from the mantle cavity — when they want to move quickly, they squirt a jet of water out through the nozzle, propelling them in the opposite direction.

Only a few of the 650 or so species of cephalopods produce shells, but some produce "quills," such as the squid, and others — for example the cuttlefish — produce a "bone." Many do not construct any hard parts that would be considered to have a place in a shell collection. Even so, they are a fascinating group worthy of study.

*Class Gastropoda (univalves) — Snail Shells*
The gastropods are a vast group of about 60,000 species, covering habitats in the sea, on land, and in fresh water. They produce a single shell, which is coiled in a spiral, just like a garden snail — this is not surprising, as snails are gastropods themselves! The exceptions to this are the slugs, which as we have seen earlier are true mollusks. As with the garden snail, most are able to withdraw into the shell when threatened, and some have a horny operculum to add to this defensive capability. They feed using a structure called the radula — this is a sort of "rasping tongue," which looks like a mechanical conveyor belt with small bucket-like teeth on it when seen under a microscope.

The species of gastropods that live on land use the operculum mostly to reduce moisture loss during extended periods of inactivity, such as during the winter or in times of unusual heat. The smallest species are very small, being only 0.02in long (0.5mm), whereas the biggest species are huge — up to 30in long (760mm)!

The gastropods divide up into four main groups: the Archaeogastropods, Neogastropods, Mesogastropods, and Tectibranchs.

The Archaeogastropods include the True Limpets (Patellidae), the Keyhole Limpets (Fissurellidae), the Abalones (Haliotidae), the Turbans (Turbinidae), the Top Shells (Trochidae), the Slit Shells (Pleurotomariidae), and the Nerites (Neritidae).

The Neogastropods include the Volutes (Volutidae), the Olives

(Olividae), the Cones (Conidae), the Murex and Rock Shells (Muricidae), the Mitres (Mitridae), the Whelks and Melongenas (Melongenidae), the Tulip Shells (Fasciolariidae), the Margin Shells (Marginellidae), the Turrid Shells (Turridae), the Nutmegs (Cancellariidae), the Augers (Turitellidae), and the Vases (Vasidae).

The Mesogastropods include the Cowries (Cypraeidae), the Wentletraps (Epitonidae), the Periwinkles (Littorinidae), the Slipper Shells (Calyptraeidae), the True Conchs (Strombidae), the Helmet Shells (Cassididae), the Sundials (Xenophoridae), the Moon Snails (Naticidae ), the Tritons (Cymatiidae), the Frog Shells (Bursidae), the Tuns (Tonnidae), and the Ceriths (Cerithiidae).

The Tectibranchs include the Bubble Shells (Bullidae).

*Class Pelecypoda (bivalves) — Oysters, Clams, etc.*

**Far Right: Scallop shells are often highly colored, as can be seen here.**

Most of the 10,000 or so species of bivalves are marine, but there are also many hundreds of species that live in fresh water — there are, however, no species that live on land. The family is one of extremes when it comes to size — the smallest bivalves are very small, about 0.02in long (0.5mm), and the largest are very big indeed at about 4ft (1.3m) across.

Bivalves are characterized by having two halves, known as "valves." These open along a hinge-line, and are held together by a ligament. They mostly filter their food from the water around them, hence they don't have the "rasping tongue" known as the radula. They use their gills both for respiration and as the "net" for filtering their food.

There are many groups within the class, including the following families: Ark Shells (Arcidae), Bittersweets (Glycymerididae), Cockles (Cardiidae), Giant Clams (Tridacnidae), Lucinas (Lucinacea), Mussels (Mytilidae), Pearl Oysters (Pteriidae), Pens (Pinnidae), Piddocks (Pholadidae), Razor Shells (Solenidae), Scallops (Pectinidae), Surf Clams (Mactridae), Tellin Clams (Tellinidae), Thorny Oysters (Spondylidae), Venus Clams (Veneridae), Watering Pots (Clavigellidae).

*Micro-Mollusks*

When establishing a shell collection, there is a question that you will have to face sooner or later, and that is whether you are going to include micro-mollusks. One of the best ways of acquiring them is to purchase bags of gravel from various beaches around the world — it's then down to you to sort through it all and separate the shells from the grit. There is no real difference between a micro-mollusk and its macro version — apart from size. The larger micros are about 0.2in (5mm) long, with the smaller ones going down to about 0.03in (0.75mm).

# The evolution of shells

**In the right places, many fossils can be found — although to come across something as spectacular as this ammonite would take a lot of searching unless you're very lucky.**

The history of shells stretches back over 500 million years, during which time a huge number of different species has evolved. Every possible habitat has its mollusk representatives with the major exception of the air: there are no flying shell species, although there are several that jump!

The mechanisms of evolution have been the subject of intense study for several hundred years, since at least the times of ancient Greece. The name of Charles Darwin will, of course, be forever linked with his theories of natural selection, but it was his grandfather, Erasmus, who first put the family name into the arena of evolutionary science. Another great scientist who made a massive contribution to the study of shells was Jean-Baptiste Pierre-Antoine de Lamarck. His ideas concerning evolution were centered around "acquired characteristics," whereas Darwin's proposed the "survival of the fittest." Although Lamarck was from a minor aristocratic family, he spent most of his life devoted to the study of science. He died penniless, however, thanks to the hostility of certain powerful scientists, and was buried in an unmarked pauper's grave. It was a sad end to a man who made many great contributions to science.

Lamarck's problem was that his ideas challenged the very foundations of Christianity, still the dominant force in academic circles throughout the western world — Napoleon is said to have told his biologists "Do not meddle with my Bible!" The same worries troubled Darwin for many years: although by the mid-Victorian era, the scientific community was well established and was on the brink of discoveries that would revolutionize mankind's view of the world, academia was still held back by the grip of dogma. This perspective received a mortal blow when Darwin finally published *The Origin Of Species* in 1859. He had written it years before, but, worried about being ostracized from his circle of scientific study, he did not dare publish until persuaded by some of his eminent friends. They were worried that Alfred Russel Wallace would get his work on the same subject in print before Darwin.

Modern-day perspectives of Lamarck's work are skewed by two powerful factors: first the Darwinists, whose hero-worship spurns any ideas that do not come directly from their idol (although Darwin himself held Lamarck in the highest standing). A second issue is that Lamarckism was taken up by the communists, whose interpretation of his work provided for a greater evolutionary equality among people. In other words, if you entertain the concepts suggested by Lamarck, you are often perceived as being a communist, and also further risk being ridiculed by the Darwinists who still dominate the study of biology.

There is the chance, however, that some of Lamarck's ideas will make a comeback. Up until now the strongest argument against acquired characteristics is that there is no real change in the DNA molecule from formation of the embryo, through to death. In other words, there is no

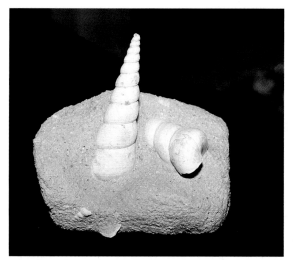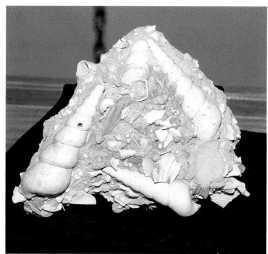

way for any changes in the lifestyle of an organism to be passed on to its offspring. However, the mechanism for this change may exist after all at the sub-atomic level, but in a manner we have not been able to (and still can't!) prove or disprove. If the DNA molecule were to have information written on it (such as instinct) in a manner that followed the possibilities of quantum computation, then Lamarck would have been right after all!

No matter the finer points of certain aspects of evolution, there are few who would argue with the major mechanisms such as the divergence of species through geographical or geophysical isolation. In other words, one species can become two different ones over a long period of time as a result of them becoming separated by a river, desert, or some other natural barrier. The classic demonstration of this is with Darwin's finches on the various Galapagos Islands — these started out with one common ancestor, but due to being on islands with differing environmental conditions, they gradually became more and more different until they could no longer inter-breed — which is the classic measure of species separation.

This happens in the world of shells as well as with birds, except the barriers tend to be things like abyssal trenches, often caused by geological events. We still have a lot to discover about the population distributions and habits of shell species in comparison to terrestrial organisms, although given the practical considerations of studying animals in deep water, this is not surprising.

One of the other problems that will not surprise anyone who has studied shells for any length of time is that some species are so variable that until a great number of them have been examined, it is close to impossible to describe them properly. A good example of this is with many of the cowry species, where over the years, taxonomists have almost been at war with each other!

**The history of mollusc evolution is well represented in the fossil record — these turritellas date from around 100 million years ago, and have closely related species living today.**

# Shells in the fossil record

The evolution of shelled mollusks is well represented in the fossil record because the shells have survived well — at least in comparison to animals with soft bodies, such as butterflies. On the right beaches there are more mollusk fossils in a single handful of gravel than the entire number of documented butterfly fossils ever found (less than fifty).

The process of turning from a shell into a fossil is straightforward; the aragonite crystals are simply transformed into calcite over geologic time, creating a fossil. The result of this calcification is that we are left with very detailed three-dimensional structures to examine, allowing us to learn far more about them than most other fossils, which typically end up as flat imprints. The soft parts of the mollusk are completely lost, but for those species that have relatives alive today, we can work out quite accurately the arrangements of these tissues. Those that have no modern counterparts are, however, much more difficult to interpret.

Shells first make an appearance in the fossil record about 500 million years ago, in the Lower Cambrian period, but we can be pretty sure that there were even older precursors to these. Apart from the aplacophorans, all the classes of mollusks are represented in the fossil record. This can be helpful in the study of today's shells, because it can be easier to study deep water mollusks from fossils rather than from life. This is because movements of the earth's crust over vast periods of geological time have thrust previously deep water environments upward so that today we can find fossilized sea shells on dry land, allowing much easier access than abyssal trench habitats.

The cephalopods are one of the few groups not doing as well today as they have in the past, with the members of the genus nautilus being the only surviving species of the subclass Nautiloidea. Perhaps the most famous of cephalopod fossils are the ammonites, which are members of the subclass Ammonoidea. These died out completely at more or less the same time as the dinosaurs, at the end of the Cretaceous period, some 60 million years ago — whether this was due to the same cause or not, we don't know.

Extremely successful for around 250 million years, ammonites are to be found in fossil deposits almost everywhere, varying in size tremendously. The smallest are less than 0.25in (6mm) across, the biggest are up to 6.5ft (2m) in diameter! Sometimes they are found as calcified remains, but in other places they instead became "pyritized," which means that rather than turning into calcite, they are composed of iron pyrites. This is a famous mineral, known to many as "fool's gold," because it looks very similar to the valuable metal. The result is that it is possible to find ammonite fossils that look as though they have been cast in bronze!

One of the problems with the study of the ammonites is that they did not become fossils where they died — their shells were light and could

have been washed considerable distances before they finally became part of the sedimentary deposits. This makes it impossible to make inferences from the locations of the fossils that we find today. We do know, however, that they were a major part of the food chain, being a constituent part of the diet of many larger animals. We know this because their remains have been found in the stomachs of marine reptilian predators of the era. It is likely that the soft parts of an ammonite's body were similar to that of the nautilus, but we cannot tell this from fossils. No matter what toll the predation took on their numbers, for them to have survived in such huge and diverse populations for 250 million years makes them one of the great success stories of the natural world.

Fossil shells can be very useful for dating rock strata, and also establishing from which type of habitat a particular rock formation came. When shell species are found that didn't undergo "post-mortem transportation" (movement of the shell due to waves, floatation, etc.) we can work out from what we know about their living relatives what the environment must have been like. For instance, it is not difficult to work out that if you find fossil limpets or abalones, they were living in rocky coastal waters — they simply don't exist anywhere else.

For shell collectors, fossils may or may not be significant. For someone who collects a very specific group of shells, only having their modern-day representatives may make the story incomplete, so it would make a lot of sense to include their ancestors. For the general collector though, perhaps the only justification for studying fossils is that it will improve the understanding of why modern shells look like they do.

**Above: Ammonites vary in size from those that can only be seen through a magnifying glass, to those that measure more than two feet across.**

**Below: Marine fossils come in all shapes and sizes — these are orthoceras, belonging to the cephalopods and so counting as mollusks. They became extinct a very long time ago so their structure can only be guessed at.**

# The life cycle

The life stories of mollusks are complex, particularly those species that live in water — terrestrial mollusks are more limited in their possibilities. The simplest life cycles are those where eggs are laid, from which the young hatch, and then proceed to grow into adults. Some species even retain their eggs until the young shells hatch out as miniature adults.

While there are many thousands of species where a "typical" life-cycle happens, there are countless numbers where the story is much more interesting — and many species where the entire process is completely unknown, as we only have found the adult form. Where this is the case, it is usually because the dead shell has been brought up from some great depth, so we don't even know whether this was its original habitat, or whether it started out at a higher level.

Those people who collect from beaches or by diving will be familiar with eggcases, often of mollusks, although sometimes it is difficult to tell. Many of the cartilaginous fishes, such as sharks, rays (sometimes called banjo sharks), and dogfish produce strange-shaped cases. Mostly the cases are empty — the young having hatched successfully before their attachments were broken during a storm or through direct disturbance, such as from a ship's anchors or trawl nets. The purpose of the cases is to provide a safe environment for the young until they are strong enough to make their own way. Sometimes the cases are produced singly, sometimes in long strings, or "egg-masses."

The fertilization of mollusk eggs is chancy. Adult females release them directly into the water and the males then release their sperm (known as "milt") in the same way. The mechanism used to ensure synchronization is sometimes through a hormone released by the females, and other times it is via phases of the moon — mostly though, we just don't know.

Different species of shells spawn at different times of year: for instance, the Blue Mussel (*Mytilus edulis*) does so in the spring, whereas the Great Scallop (*Pecten maximus*) spawns in the summer. The shell species that release their eggs and milt directly into the water consign the vast majority of them to become food for a huge number of other organisms. In order to overcome these losses, they produce incredible numbers: the female Blue Mussel may produce up to 12 million eggs.

Some species complicate the picture of mollusk breeding habits even further. Take the Great Scallop, which has both male and female sexual organs. The release of their eggs and milt are staggered to maximize the chance of them being fertilized by other individuals. This helps to ensure that some degree of genetic diversity is maintained.

Once the eggs have hatched, there is no set pattern for their development — some join briefly the massive swarms of planktonic life, during which time they will run the risk of being eaten by everything from barnacles to whales. Sooner or later, though, they settle down and begin

**Below: The seashore card series shows a razor shell, limpets, and the egg case of a blonde ray.**

to grow into adults. Some will attach themselves to rocks, seaweed, or some other such substrate, while others will stay free-living.

When shells first hatch, they sometimes go through an intermediate stage known as a "trochophore"; after this they develop into a "veliger," which is the larval form of mollusks. They may well go through more than one stage of veliger, as with the American Oyster. If they are of a species that attaches itself to some fixed structure, they will be under pressure not only from other individuals of the same species, but also from many other organisms — barnacles, seaweed, algae, sea anemones, and so on. Some species, such as certain mussels, are able to detach themselves while they are young, and move a short distance in an attempt to find a more suitable site. Most others are unable to do this.

There are many more interesting aspects of mollusks' life cycles than there is space to describe here. Some have the strangest relationships and interactions with all manner of other organisms: for example, some species' veligers are parasitic on fish.

Mollusks feed on a wide variety of different things — some are herbivores, grazing on algae, seaweed, etc. Species which do this include those in the Class Monoplacophora, the Class Polyplacophora, and the Class Gastropoda. In other words, the list of herbivorous shell species contains the chitons, the limpets, the snails (land, marine, and freshwater), abalones, and so on. Other mollusks are carnivorous, feeding on all sorts of prey. Many, such as the Murex shells, favor attacking other shells and they can become pests of commercially farmed species, such as oysters. However, the large proportion of mollusk species are filter feeders; these include oysters and mussels, as well as all the other bivalves.

The main source of food obtained from filtering activities are the myriad organisms which make up the planktonic hordes. Among these, a vast number are diatoms, which teem in fresh water and marine environments. These microscopic plants are a sort of unicellular algae which have silica as a component of their cell walls. Some live singly, others in colonies. They contain chlorophyll, which, combined with their vast numbers, means that they play a vital part in the maintenance of the planet's ecosystem. It has been estimated they remove around a quarter of all the carbon dioxide from the earth's atmosphere! Diatoms are a vital part of the food-chain: life as we know it in the oceans would not be possible without them. They are also varied in their lifestyles: some are free floaters in the oceans; others attach themselves to all manner of objects.

The other major category of feeding habit are detritus feeders such as the aplacophorans. Detritus is the word given to the organic debris which has resulted from the decomposition of plants and animals. Many mollusks have evolved to specialize in this source of nutrition, especially those herbivores which live in the depths of the oceans.

*Patella safiana* **is a typical limpet, of which there are about 400 species. These herbivorous mollusks are well known for their habit of clinging to rocks, piers, jetties, and almost any other stationary object in the tidal zones of the world. They use a very strong muscular foot to clamp themselves to their chosen rest site. When the tide is in, they move around grazing on algae and other small plants, only returning to their rest location as the water recedes.**

# Pests, predators, parasites, pollutants and preservation

When one thinks about pests, mollusks — at least marine ones — are not usually the first to spring to mind. There are, however, some that cost the economies of some countries huge amounts to overcome. The issue of slugs and snails destroying agricultural crops is so well known as to be not worth discussing here. A less well known problem was created when the Zebra Mussel (*Dreissena polymorpha*) was introduced to North America by accident in the late 1980s. This European species established itself rapidly, causing massive problems due to the way it blocks water pipes, such as those used for water treatment plants and for industrial sites. It is spreading rapidly throughout its newly-found continental home, partly by attaching itself to boats, but also by its very effective reproductive techniques. These involve the release of spawn and milt, which later develop into free-swimming planktonic larvae in much the same manner as their marine cousins.

Represented among the thousands of species of mollusks, there are both predators and parasites. There are also species which fall victim to all manner of predators and parasites — to complicate the subject still further, there are others which play a vital part in the life-cycles of non-molluskan parasites.

As prey, marine and freshwater mollusks form an important part in the diet of all sorts of creatures, from other shells through to fish, crabs, starfish, diving birds, and even otters. Those mollusks of tidal regions also fall victim to the attentions of a variety of terrestrial predators when low, tide exposes them. These animals include other bird species, racoons, mink, foxes, and many other often surprising species.

Land mollusks fall victim to almost every possible predator species, although some of these predators get more than they bargained for: many terrestrial mollusks are used as vectors by parasites. To give an example, the liver-fluke flatworm infects certain snails which live in the grasses of water meadows. When these get eaten accidentally by animals like sheep, cattle, and goats, the flatworms work their way into the liver and bile-ducts of their new host, causing severe illness and death.

One of the consequences of having developed hard shells is that mollusks are well protected against most predators. There are, however, some animals that have either evolved physical structures that enable them to get through this protection, or have developed behavioral methods. Those in the first category include the Murex shells which use a combination of mechanical action and powerful digestive juices in order to gain entry to the soft tissues of their mollusk victims. The second category typically uses some form of tool to break through the shell. Mankind obviously falls into this group, the most delightful of which are the sea-otters of the North American coasts. By some means they have discovered that they can break mollusk shells against flat stones while in the water. They do so floating on their backs, with the stone positioned on their belly. They then strike the shell repeatedly against the improvized anvil until the shell gives way, and they can get at the food inside. Unfortunately, the fondness of otters for mollusks is a major cause for worry. Since the mollusks are nearly all filter feeders, they build up levels of toxins in their body tissues. These, generally, are not a problem to the mollusk as the quantities involved are very small. The danger comes when a larger organism, such as an otter, eats large numbers of these shells — the toxins then build up in the body resulting in all sorts of problems.

The toxins found in marine environments are often compounds of heavy metals such as mercury or, more commonly in inshore waters, tin. These are used as anti-fouling agents in marine paints, in the form of tributyl tin — often called "TBT." The use of tin for this purpose is now prohibited in many countries because of its toxicity to the environment. The problem is that it stays in the ecosystem for a very long time, which coupled with the large quantities of it still on boats all over the world, means that there is still an awful lot of it yet to flake off and fall into the mud and sand of inshore waters. This means that it will be a very long time before we are free of this particular contaminant.

This has been just the briefest of looks at the very complicated subjects of predation, parasitism, and pollution. Each of these could easily be the study of an entire lifetime, so a paragraph or two is never going to be adequate! If you want to learn more about them, there are thousands of excellent publications available, either from bookstores, libraries, or on the internet.

The issues of preservation and conservation are guaranteed to provoke passionate reactions from numerous people, many of whom are decidedly militant against collecting of any sort of animal or plant. Unfortunately, these extremists are causing divisions within just about every branch of natural science, at a time when we all ought to be concentrating on the bigger picture — that of habitat loss, pollution and the over-commercialization of many ecosystems.

A good example of over-exploitation has been repeated many times over the world with the over-fishing of certain species. One of the most famous occurred when the anchovy was fished off the coast of South America. It was once so plentiful that huge colonies of birds were supported by them, but when man moved in with massive trawlers, they were all but wiped out — first the fish and then the birds followed due to starvation. The same thing happened in the North Sea, between England and Holland, where enormous shoals of herring supplied a large industry devoted to their capture and processing. These days the North Sea hasn't seen a herring boat for years.

I used these examples because the results are so visible, but sadly

**Pressure on mollusk species can come from all sorts of directions. The Tusk shells, for instance, were once used as currency by the native American Indian tribes of the Pacific Northwest. Many common foreign Tusk shells were imported into America by unscrupulous traders in order to exchange them with Indian tribes for furs and other goods. This one, the Vernede's Tusk, is from eastern Asia.**

This pile of cowries was photographed in Hawaii, USA — it is collecting on this scale that threatens the survival of many species of mollusk all over the world.

many shell species are going the same way. In the Far East little concern was given to the over-fishing of declining species for a long time — some countries have changed their attitudes in the recent past, and are working hard to monitor the situation. As a result they restrict collection licences where necessary until stocks have built up again.

It is not just third-world countries that are guilty of plundering declining stocks of mollusk species. The Great Scallop (*Pecten maximus*), for instance, is heavily over-fished in many areas, and is declining in numbers as a consequence. One of the biggest problems is the way that scallop trawling is done — massive "dredges" or "drags" are towed across the sea-bed. The scallop normally digs itself into the sand or mud, so the dredges have to rake this in order to dislodge the scallops so that the following net can capture them. Sadly, the damage done to the sea-bed is immense, and it rarely gets the chance to recover before another boat runs a dredge through the same area. This also destroys the habitat for just about every other animal and plant species present. Many once productive scallop grounds are marine deserts these days — devoid of any significant life at all.

Once it is accepted that there are serious threats to the environment generally, the next question to address is what can be done to help endangered species and, in the context of this book, specifically mollusks. Most conservation projects start with conserving the habitat — it is no use trying to save a species from extinction if it has nowhere to live. Many shell species live on coral reefs, and as these are one of the most endangered and most visible of habitats, we will look at them in more detail.

One of the biggest problems with trying to implement conservation policies in marine habitats, is that nearly all of the human threats come from sources that are either unidentifiable, or extremely difficult to prove, making enforcement next to impossible. These threats range from the careless use of boat anchors, which can rip up large pieces of coral — when taken over a period of time the large numbers of boats that frequent the reefs can create a lot of damage.

There are many other sources of damage to coral that are directly attributable to human activity — some of which are potentially easy to rectify, whereas others will take a lot of effort to sort out. A good example of the former is the collecting of coral by local divers for sale to tourists. The easy solution would be to ban the sale and collection of coral. This has been done in some countries, but there are many that have yet to follow suit. There are social issues that need addressing, however, when this sort of policy is set in motion — if you stop the divers from making a living like this, you need to find a viable alternative if the measures are going to last.

Coral reefs do get damaged by natural events such as hurricanes, but it is the ever-increasing human population that is causing by far the biggest worry for conservationists. When you have more people in a society, there is obviously a lot of pressure to house them in some way. These demands usually have precedence in political circles over conservation, especially in the third world where so many of the valuable habitats are located. As a consequence of this, there are huge numbers of development projects under way all over the world.

These building developments add to the problem of waste outflows into rivers and seas, especially where the sewage treatment is rudimentary or non-existent. The result is several threats to coral: the increase in suspended nutrients can favor other organisms and reduce the amount of light reaching the reefs. Both of these are bad news, but as if this wasn't enough, the extra population attracted by the nutrients fishes the reefs harder and harder, until the coral dies. The collapse of local ecosystems has effectively killed vast areas of reefs throughout the world.

For fisherman, reefs pose quite a problem, because they are not suited to the use of trawl nets, which get entangled and ruined. Often there are too few big fish left to make line fishing viable, so some try "human ingenuity" instead. Personally, I think vandalism is a better word, as they use poisons and explosives to stun the fish so that they can be collected by hand off the surface. It is no surprise that both are really destructive to the coral as well as the fish stocks.

One of the most unlikely threats to the survival of some Pacific coral reefs is a starfish. This is the Crown-of-Thorns (*Acanthaster planci*), and it is threat for two basic reasons — first, it eats cora; second, it reproduces extremely prolifically, resulting in regular explosions in numbers. Every time there is a boom in Crown-of-Thorns' numbers, they do huge amounts of damage to whichever reef they are occupying. Quite why the starfish is being so successful is the subject of much discussion and research, but suggestions include human causes such as increased nutrient levels, pollution, and so on.

Coral reefs are just one of many habitats that face massive losses if we do not attempt to redress the balances we have upset so badly. Others have been detailed elsewhere in this book, such as the delicately balanced and vulnerable freshwater systems, which are perhaps the most threatened of all. There is no easy answer to the problem of conserving endangered animal and plant species, and protecting their habitats is just the first step on the way to doing this.

# Habitats

*Ocean surface or "Pelagic" habitats*
When people think of where shells live, they rarely think of them floating on the sea's surface, but in fact there are quite a few species — about 100 in all — that spend the greater part of their lives in just this manner. Most of them attach themselves to things that float, such as the various species of seaweeds that grow on or near the surface.

*Inter-tidal or "Littoral" habitats*
Marine habitats can be divided up into zones. The first of these is the zone which lies between the high and low tide marks. This is called by several names, including the tidal, inter-tidal, or littoral zone. The scientific term for the animals and plants that live in this zone is "littoral species."

There are a great many mollusk species which specialize in inhabiting the littoral zone — these include limpets, periwinkles, mussels, oysters, and so on. Most of them, however, also overlap with the shallower regions of the "sub-littoral" zone, which is the next one down, in terms of depth.

The littoral zone can be further divided up by the type of terrain a specific location is comprised of, such as mud flats, sand flats, gravel beaches, rocky areas, mangrove swamps, and so on. Each of these subdivisions has its own particular fauna and flora, or "biota," as biologists would call it.

The species that inhabit mud and sand flats are many and diverse. Massive colonies of mussels establish themselves in some of these locations, as do oysters. They then provide a suitable environment for other mollusk species, especially those that prey on these colonial aggregations, such as murex, whelks, and chanks. The rich supply of nutrients found in the mud flats can sustain enormous numbers of some of the smaller mollusk species, such as the Spire shell, which is about 0.25in (64mm) long. This has been found to number over 40,000 individuals in a square meter!

Many of the shells that inhabit mud and sand flats live singly, such as the burrowing species — these include razor shells, cockles, clams, tellins, and the "grazers," such as conches. These also fall victim to the same sorts of predatory mollusks mentioned above.

The greatest diversity of mollusk species in the littoral zone is found in the rocky areas. This is because there are so many ecological niches available there, such as in rock pools, amongst seaweed, under stones, on rocks, in crevices, and so on. Probably the most immediately obvious are the limpets, which attach themselves to rocks in the full view of any observer. Periwinkles can be found hiding amongst fronds of seaweed, and any other convenient hiding places.

The predatory mollusks are fewer in number than the herbivorous species (as they are everywhere), but are nevertheless still present in

**Whenever you see piles of cockle shells washed up on a beach, you can be certain that there is a very large bed of them nearby.**

rocky environments. It would be seriously bad news if the predators out-numbered their prey, as it would mean both would die out very quickly.

*Shallow water or "Sub-littoral" habitats*
Immediately below the littoral, is the "sub-littoral" zone. This is formed by the region which runs from the low water mark to the edge of the continental shelf. This is the area of land that would be exposed if the sea level fell by say, a 1,000ft (300m). In other words, it is the continuation of the existing continents as far as the point where they drop off into deep water. It is a region of great diversity in terms of numbers of species of both plants and animals, and mollusks are no exception. Where the local ecology has not been destroyed by over-fishing, pollution, or any of mankind's other activities, the sub-littoral zone is normally rich in numbers of all manner of marine organisms, including most mollusk species.

One of the richest of all maritime habitats is the coral reef, where the good light levels, combined with high water temperatures provide the best possible environment for marine life. Coral is constructed by communal polyps, which are small animals which are similar to small sea anemones. They are, however, part plants, in that within their bodies are large numbers of algae cells. These are used in a mutually beneficial relationship, such that the algae get somewhere safe to live, and are supplied with nutrient in the form of the polyps' waste products. The polyps in return get oxygen released within their bodies, allowing them to survive.

Coral reefs are constructed from limestone which is secreted by the polyps all their lives, but only the outer skin of it is actually still living — the rest is composed of dead polyp chambers made by earlier generations. The reef's complex shapes provide hiding places for countless numbers of other animals and plants, most of which have evolved to fit in very closely with the ecosystem thus created.

The coral polyps themselves are treated as food by all sorts of creatures — parrot fish, for instance, have massively powerful jaws, which enables them to bite pieces of coral from the reef, and then crunch it up to extract any goodness held within. One of the animals that can represent a real threat to entire coral reefs — as mentioned earlier — is the starfish, which can secrete a fluid which dissolves the limestone, allowing them to get at the tasty polyp inside.

There are many thousands of mollusk species which inhabit coral reefs, and some of these, such as clams, actually bore their way into the coral, and live there permanently. Many other animals use holes in the reefs to hide in as well — the deeper ones may hold lurking moray eels, lobsters, crabs, fish, and so on. The areas of rubble around living coral can be very productive for shells, usually supporting more species than the coral itself.

**There is no telling what treasures a pile of shells such as this might hold!**

*Deep sea habitats*

At the edge of the continental shelf, there is a slope which runs down into the deep abyss; the majority of the world's oceans are comprised of this sort of terrain — the average depth of the ocean around the world is 2.5 miles (4km). The deepest places are in the trenches — the record is held by the Mariana Trench, at about 36,000ft, which is nearly 7.5 miles (11.7km). Many of the animals and plants that inhabit the depths are very strange when compared with their shallow water counterparts, especially some of the species of fish. The mollusks are probably the most "normal" of all the inhabitants of the depths.

The species of shells which live in deep water habitats have two main environmental factors that separate them from those of shallow seas. These are temperature, and light — or should I say temperature and dark, because no light whatsoever penetrates below about 3,000ft (900m). The temperature is usually just above freezing point — it gets this low because warm water is lighter than cold, so it rises, leaving the depths very cold. There is also a huge "thermal inertia" in the oceans, which means that the range of temperature fluctuations is very small — this is because water has a very high thermal capacity. It takes a lot of energy to raise the temperature of even a small amount of water by a few degrees, so when it comes to cubic miles of water, it is no surprise that they are very stable.

There are exceptions to deep water being so cold, such as in the depths of the Red Sea and the Mediterranean where temperatures are much higher. There are, however, localized zones where temperatures are extremely high — in the vicinity of hydrothermal vents. These occur where there is deep sea volcanic activity, and are formed when water seeps into cracks it forms in the sea bed.

The water which does this becomes "super-heated," which means that it is well above boiling point (sometimes in excess of 850°F/440°C); this is made possible by the extreme pressures created by the tons of water bearing down on every square inch. Water pressure increases by about 15lb/sq in (000kg/sq cm) for every 35ft (10.5m) in depth. Consequently, by the time you have gone down, say, 6,000ft (1,800m), you have a pressure of about 2,500lb/sq in (000kg/sq cm)!

This extreme pressure is not a problem to marine creatures from an engineering point of view, because they are at the same pressure inside as out: in other words, they are at a sort of equilibrium. They don't therefore have to build massive shells to resist the pressure. It does, however, affect the rate of the chemical processes that control the metabolic systems that keep the organisms alive, so they have had to evolve different ways to cope with it.

The raised temperatures, combined with the release of hydrogen sulphide (always present with any volcanic activity), result in prolific ecosystems around every hydrothermal vent. Other minerals produced by the geological processes also help to provide a habitat that is a distinct improvement over the barren wastes that form the majority of the sea-bed at increased depths.

The large amount of hydrogen sulphide creates a good environment for certain types of bacteria, which then abound. These form the vital basis for a food-chain, which includes many mollusks. The fact that no light reaches the depths means that any shells that live there must either be scavengers, parasites, or predators — there is no plant life in total dark-ness, so there are no herbivorous grazing species living there. There are non-grazing herbivores, but they all feed on vegetative material that orig-inated at or near the surface, and has sunk through the depths to accu-mulate on the seabed. This is mostly soft mud, which is the result of mil-lions of years of sediment and detritus falling from the surface waters.

When compared to shallower waters, there is a higher proportion of scavenging mollusks at great depths. They subsist off almost any material that falls from activity nearer the surface. Much of this results from the outflow of rivers, which deposit vast quantities of organic material into the oceans. Most of this ends up on the continental shelves, but in some areas, it reaches the deep as well. Extra supplies of such material results from the action of severe weather at the surface, such as typhoons, tor-nadoes, storms, and so on.

*Freshwater habitats*
Molluscs are very successful in the majority of the world's fresh waters, although surprisingly only two classes have made the transition from salt water — the bivalves and the gastropods. Quite why the others do not seem to have ever done so is not known, something about bivalves and gastropods obviously makes them more able to make the cross-over.

Throughout the evolution of mollusks there are many examples of species moving from one environment to another, such as from the sea to the land. Of those that live in fresh water, some came directly from the sea, but others first went via the land. As the only class of mollusks to become terrestrial are the gastropods, we are talking exclusively about various types of snail.

We can often determine which route a particular species took by its current form — most land species did away with their operculae, which are the "trapdoor" devices used to keep out predators. This is because while strong shells and operculae work well in the sea, they have disad-vantages on land, the main one of which is that they are heavy. This is not an issue in water because it effectively makes them weigh less. On land though, it is a big problem, as it is more important to be able to move

**The Ram's Horn Snail —** *Planorbis corneus* **— is a freshwater species from the Planorbis genus, which translates to "flat spiral." They live in a variety of ponds and lakes which often have very low oxygen levels. To cope with this they have evolved a very efficient blood system which is based on haemoglobin — this makes their blood a red color which is very similar to that of mammals.**

than it is to be well defended. As a consequence, land mollusks have modified the operculum by reducing it to a tough corneous membrane.

In addition to changes to the operculum, most land mollusks have also modified the way that they breathe. Instead of doing so through a gill structure, they usually breathe through a form of lung which evolved out of mantle tissue. So we have two immediate ways to assess whether a freshwater species came from the land or the sea — if it breathes through a gill and has a calcareous operculum, it is definitely directly from a marine ancestor, whereas if it has the characteristics of a land shell, then it is probable that this is where it came from.

The various species of freshwater mollusks do not grow as big as their marine cousins, but even so they still vary in size within quite a wide spectrum. The smallest species are quite similar to those of salt water, but the largest is the freshwater mussel (*Megalonaias nervosa*), which reaches nearly a foot in length (280mm). They are also more restricted in their feeding habits than marine shells, with most being either grazers or filter-feeders.

One of the problems that face freshwater mollusks is that due to their restricted and specific habitats, they are very vulnerable to the actions of mankind, especially from pollution. An example is the potentially lethal threat posed when destructive farming, industrial or mining activities release quantities of effluents into rivers. This can reduce the oxygen content to levels below that at which most organisms can survive, including mollusks. For species which are already struggling to maintain an existence, this can be the final blow before extinction occurs.

Land Or "Terrestrial" Habitats

As mentioned above all terrestrial or land mollusks are in the Class Gastropoda, making them snails of one sort or another. They have all developed out of marine ancestors, and have reduced their operculae to corneous membranes, which are used primarily to retain moisture, but also for defense. They have also modified their breathing mechanisms from gill-type structures to primitive lungs out of modified mantle tissues. The most significant difference to mollusks, however, is that when they are out of water, they do not have the assistance of water's inherent buoyancy to compensate for their unusually high mass. Another feature which separates land mollusks from others is that they have evolved to be able to reproduce away from either salt or fresh water.

If marine mollusks were to try and move around on land with shells of the same thickness and weight as they have under water, they would be too heavy to move around effectively. They would also have to face up to the fact that in a lot of habitats there is very little calcium available to be metabolized into shell-making materials. I would suspect, therefore,

that evolution would pretty quickly favor those species which put their resources into producing higher numbers of young instead of those which built thick shells.

There are vast numbers of different terrestrial mollusk species — something like 45,000, which is a good illustration of how successful they have been over the 350 million or so years that they have been on land. They have evolved to survive in all sorts of diverse environments, even deserts in some cases. Most are, however, quite habitat specific — that is, they have adapted to compete in a particular type of environment, which then means that they are tied to it.

Many of these species can be really difficult to iidentify though, as their patterns and coloration can be notoriously variable. This means that to get a thorough understanding of how one species differs from another might require years of research. This may seem a little pointless to the uninitiated, but when you consider, for instance, the significance of how dangerous parasites might associate with one species of mollusk, but not another, it suddenly takes on a fresh importance.

One of the first reasons that land mollusks were studied in any detail is that many of them are edible. The high nutritional value of snails means that they have been recognized as a good food source for a long time. This encouraged early civilizations to find out how to raise them in captivity. Quite when they were first farmed, we don't know, but it must have been a very long time ago, as their remains have been found during archaeological excavations of prehistoric man.

There are detailed descriptions by Pliny, of how in ancient Rome snails were kept for this purpose. Incidentally, farming them is called "Heliciculture." Snails are still eaten to this day in many parts of the world. The French are especially renowned for their partiality to them as a delicacy, and are reputed to be responsible for introducing the brown garden snail to the United States in the 1850s.

**Garden snails are not the only shelled mollusks to be found out of water — the African giant land snail (Achatina fulica) shown here is one of the bigger species and can grow to over 4in (100mm).**

# Establishing a shell collection

For those people new to shells, establishing a collection may be their primary goal. This can be achieved in many ways, but there are several factors that will influence the best choice of methods. The acquisition of shells basically divides into two methods — finding them yourself, or getting them from someone else. The latter will typically involve either exchanging shells that are surplus to your requirements, or parting with money.

If you live a long way from the sea, and you have no money, perhaps you had better consider collecting land shells first! Seriously though, if you live near the sea, then direct collecting from the beach is probably the easiest way to get started without spending money. This will give you the chance to get a feel for the subject, and to see which types of shells particularly interest you. If you have a habit of taking holidays in exotic places, then you are going to be able to make a good start on your collection, especially if you are a scuba diver.

Diving is one of the best ways to collect shells, especially if you are fortunate enough to be able to dive in tropical seas. It is an ideal opportunity to obtain photographs of the various species in their home environment. Even better is the use of video equipment, but this can be very expensive. A lot of previously unknown information can be recorded by divers with an interest in natural history — especially by those who are covering areas rarely dived on.

The condition of specimens collected from the seabed is nearly always going to surpass that of those obtained by commercial methods — so many shells have delicate spines or other structures that it is not surprising that some species are rarely seen in a perfect state. It is very important that you have local knowledge about the species you are likely to encounter — some species, especially some of the cones, have the ability to inflict very serious wounds on the unwary. This is most likely to occur with careless handling, but some can even pierce bags with ease, so find out what you are dealing with first.

A method of collecting live shells that does not require much in the way of equipment is dredging. This is done by towing a small dredge net behind a boat, but it needs to be done over sandy or muddy bottoms. If you try to pull a dredge over rocks, you're likely to get fouled up, which at best will damage the net, and at worst lose it. Once again, you need to be aware of local regulations, and if you are in an area of commercial trawlers, be very careful that you are not going to get in the way of a boat that is in the process of a trawl. They will not thank you if they have to abort several hours work.

Dredging works well in depths of up to a hundred feet or so, and depending on the mesh size of your net, you will bring up all sorts of interesting objects. Be very careful of small fish, some of which are likely

**There are many different ways of displaying shell collections. This is an economical and space-saving method. It is simply an arrangement laid out on cotton wool in wooden trays. It is vital that an accurate label is always kept with each specimen.**

to have poisonous spines — these include scorpion fish, weavers, stone fish, and so on. They are likely to be in your net because they have a habit of burying themselves just under the surface of sand or mud on the bottom — exactly where your net is going to go. Use gloves to sort through the seaweed, stones and assorted debris that you have brought to the surface. Return any living organisms that you are not going to keep as soon as possible. You may decide, however, that shrimps, prawns, and edible crabs are too tempting to return!

There are many other ways of increasing your collection, even if you live far from the sea, or you want specimens from the other side of the world. One of the best ways is to establish a system of exchange with collectors from the regions that interest you particularly. If you manage to get this going well, both you and your contact can do very well out of it, minimizing the costs, as neither of you should be making a profit.

When you send shells, do so in the manner that will ensure that they arrive in the condition that you would expect to receive them in yourself. Only send shells in perfect condition, and make sure that they have full labels, listing where and when they were found, and so on.

If you can afford to do so, you may choose to use the services of a commercial trader, but if you cannot inspect the specimens yourself, you will have to be careful about what you are buying, especially if they are rare species. It is often best to rely on dealers who are recommended to you by someone you know and trust. Before you commit yourself to a purchase over the telephone, internet, or through the post, check out other people's prices, and find out if there is any locality information. If not, make sure that the price reflects this.

Once your collection becomes established, your next problem will be storage. You will have several issues to deal with here. First, they must be kept in a manner that will prevent them from getting damaged. Second, they must not be separated from their labels. Third, they must not be allowed to deteriorate.

There are many different ways of achieving the above aims, but they depend largely on the amount of space you have, and also on the amount of money that you can spend. A good way that does not require cabinets or large outlays of money is to use stackable shallow wooden trays filled with cotton wool. The shells are then laid out on these, together with their labels. Then all you have to do is label the outside of the trays with the name of the family contained within, and you have the makings of a successful system for storing your collection.

I'm sure that if I asked ten collectors what they used to prevent their shells drying out and deteriorating, I'd get ten different replies. The easiest effective method that I know of is to use baby oil bought at the local store. Shells should be stored very carefully, or they risk falling victim to

Byrne's Disease — a common problem in Victorian collections, where corrosion and white residues were found to be destroying valuable shells. In 1899 Byrne published a paper entitled "The Corrosion of Shells in Cabinets." He decided that certain organisms were responsible, but since then other ideas have come forward, none of which are conclusive.

Whatever the mechanism is, there seem to be some very straightforward precautions. Never allow condensation to form on your shells. Do not allow direct contact between the shells and any wooden surfaces. Keep them away from solvents, and also from fumes from the kitchen.

Just how you decide to label your shells is up to you. To a certain extent, you will have the options dictated to you by the size of the shells — if you collect micros, you won't be able to write on the shells directly, and you will have to keep each in a separate compartment or container to prevent the labels getting mixed up.

If you are au fait with technology, you can store all your records in a computerized database. The golden rule when dealing with computers is to keep multiple copies of your data — and keep them in different formats. If you decide to go the computer route, you will do yourself a favor if you take the time to decide exactly what information you want to store, before you start work. Once you have a system up and running successfully, you will be able to print lists of all manner of combinations of information, which can be especially useful if you are going somewhere that might be a potential source of shells. If you have a large collection, you will never be able to remember just what you do and don't have. If you have a category on your list for the condition of each shell, you will be able to improve your collection without buying specimens that you either have already, or are inferior to ones you have.

If you are able to run a database, then you will certainly be able to use e-mail and the internet. This where things can become useful, because you can send your "want lists" to dealers and other collectors all around the world. If you want identifications it can be useful to take a photograph of the specimens under examination, get them scanned, and then e-mail them to others for discussion.

Alternatively, you can set up your own web page, which is much easier than you might expect, and put your pictures on display. If you are specializing in a specific family or location, then you can be a real help to others by putting up a web page with your knowledge for all to see. If you are having difficulty with identifying something, then you can show a picture of it and ask for help. You no longer need to be in the centre of a large metropolis to have access to specialists. The possibilities of global communication are endless.

# Collecting in the field

**This is a loose assemblage of shells seen on a beach at Cozumel, in Mexico.**

For those unfamiliar with shell collecting, it might appear that all marine species have very similar habitats because they all live in the sea. This could not be further from the truth, for there are many different environments between the high tide mark and the sub-abyssal depths. There are, for example, many different kinds of reef — from shallow rock formations and coral structures, through to the more recent artificial constructions built for coastal defences. Combine this with the extremes of temperature caused by geographical location, the complications of ocean currents, and the influence of large rivers pouring huge quantities of freshwater and associated debris into the sea, and you start to get more and more diverse environments.

No matter the specific conditions of a particular environment, a species of mollusk will have evolved to survive there. This mollusk survival feature has resulted in all manner of adaptations, reflected in the shapes, colors, and sizes of the shells they produce — and providing one of the main attractions of shell collecting: no matter how long you have been studying the subject, you will still be surprised by permutations of form that you won't have seen before.

If you decide that you are going to start collecting shells in the field, then you are going to have to think ahead. In some places, especially where you are likely to venture out onto sand banks, you are going to need good local advice about tides and other dangers such as quicksand. Mud can also be dangerous. Near where I live someone drowned when they got stuck in the mud when the tide came in — mudflats can be desolate places where this sort of thing can happen without anyone being around to help you. So if you are going anywhere that you might run into problems, take someone with you. If you are a solitary person, then take a mobile 'phone, although this won't help you if you fall in.

After a while, you will probably decide to collect at night, for many species spend the day buried and come to the surface during the hours of darkness. Safety is even more critical if you are going to do this: it is hard enough to watch the tide during the day, let alone at night. In the excitement of the moment you can easily get carried away, leaving you in trouble when you find your return route to the shore is now a raging torrent of angry seawater. For people who have not had much experience of mudflats, it can be a real shock just how fast the tide can come in — in some places it can be faster than a human can run! Think ahead and have fun in safety.

You will also need to find out whether any local regulations affect you. In some places you will be allowed to collect from the surface, but are not permitted to dig for shells, as you would then be classed as a bait collector. Other restrictions include the need for permits, or the imposition of a closed season — so find out first. Finally, don't upset the locals. Some

may take offence if they think that you are going near their bait traps and seafarers can be somewhat direct in their retribution!

When it comes to collecting from beaches, the most productive times are after storms, and at low water during spring tides. Storms often cast up large numbers of shells, and it can be great fun picking through the debris — you never know what you will find. I still remember the day our Devon beach was littered with big juicy oranges! Perhaps a freighter had lost a container in a storm, but we didn't care how they got there: the peel kept the salt water out, and they were delicious!

If you check the tide times, you may be able to time a visit to the beach to coincide with a spring tide. Twice a year — at each equinox — the tides are more extreme than usual, meaning that at low water you will gain access to areas that are not normally uncovered. This can be very productive, especially around deep water rock-pools, but be careful: wet seaweed can be very slippery, and it is only too easy to fall and break a limb, or knock yourself out cold.

If you are collecting at all seriously, you will need to record your finds on the spot, so you'll need a notebook — make sure the ink in your pen is waterproof as it is bound to get wet at some point. You should always make a separate copy of your records in case you lose the book! Many people transfer their notes to a computerized database, an excellent means of storage. When you find a shell, you can write on it directly with waterproof ink, or you can put a label into a fresh plastic bag with the shell. The most important information is the date and the location.

Today, many people are concerned about collecting living shells — and there is a vociferous, if often ill-informed, anti-collecting lobby. One solution is to photograph shells instead of taking them. I think this is an excellent idea: for too long people have concentrated on collecting the shells, with scant regard to their ecology. I do not say "don't collect" — the number of living shells taken by amateur collectors is minuscule in relation to the number killed by every storm — I just think the more we record about them the better. In many areas this sort of information is badly needed, and the day-to-day records of ordinary shell collectors can build up into an important record of the local ecology. If this data is made available to the relevant organizations (such as local conservation soci- eties), it can be used to help monitor species population fluctuations and can be instrumental in getting official assistance to help protect endan- gered habitats, which is where the real threat to mollusk species lies.

The biggest threat to habitats comes from pollution — usually an insidious build-up of heavy metal toxins, but every now and then a cata- strophic event, such as an oil spill. I live just a few miles from the busiest shipping channel in the world (the English Channel), and we regularly have shipwrecks and oil spills. Indeed, it is not so many years ago that

**Many of the larger species are threatened by over-collecting; these were photographed in the Dominican Republic.**

entire communities used to supplement their income from scavenging through wrecks — local myth has it that some even used to set false beacons to lure ships to their doom! We have got used to rescuing oiled seabirds, seal pups, and so on, and after a while things look normal again, but it is impossible to know just how far the damage has gone. Certain mollusks are used as what is known as "indicator species." This means that they are very sensitive to environmental change, and so their numbers are a good way of assessing the health of a particular habitat. Your records could make a real difference to the monitoring of both pre- and post-disaster populations.

If you find a colony of a rare species, don't take too many specimens, and keep the location to yourself and any conservation organizations you have joined. You will have to find out for yourself which of these is most suitable — some conservation groups may want to burn you at the stake if they know you are a collector!

Unfortunately, commercial collecting is a real threat to the survival of many species, especially in the Far East where many people make a living out of collecting to supply the shell trade. This is one of the real problems of conscience when it comes to purchasing rare shells — if you buy them, you are encouraging their trade, but if you don't buy them, they won't make it into your collection. So what do you do? I leave that up to you.

Many collectors use a screen or sieve when they are looking for small species in sandy or muddy terrains — the idea is that you part fill it with the material in question, and then wash it through until only solids are left, including, it is hoped, some shells. The control factor here is the size of the mesh — obviously the smaller the hole size, the smaller the objects retained will be. An effective way to work a habitat in this manner is to search for signs of life before you go digging up the entire shoreline. Some species produce distinctive casts, trails, or holes, so once you have learned to identify what you can expect to find from each, you can save yourself a lot of time.

The same techniques of using sieves works well when diving, except that you need to think ahead if you are going to stir up a lot of silt, as you won't be able to see a thing if the tide is slack. The most productive places are under rocks, or in sandy areas between coral reefs or rock outcrops.

If you are going to turn over rocks, either in pools or when diving, there are two things to remember — first, think about what might be lurking under the rock before you lift it. If you go poking your fingers underneath looking for a decent grip, you might disturb something that would rather be left alone. It may have sharp teeth, or powerful pincers, so think ahead. Second, when you have finished investigating the rock's tenants, put it back as you found it. This is because there are living on its surface many animals and plants that will die if left upside-down.

**Shells are often washed up in their thousands, but they are usually in very poor condition, as can be seen here.**

# Shells in art, history, and human society

**Sadly, it is highly unlikely that you will be fortunate enough to find a prize like this just sitting on the shoreline! Primitive civilizations have used large shells like this as trumpets for many thousands of years.**

No one knows when shell collecting started — when the ruins of Pompeii were uncovered, among the things found was a collection of shells. While this is the earliest known example, I think it is a pretty safe bet that there were many more that pre-date it. But it is not just as collectibles that shells have benefited mankind. Seafood, particularly such things as mussels, clams, and oysters, is a *stable* source of food — meaning that instead of following herds of animals in a nomadic fashion, shore-dwelling early man was able to settle and find or build more or less permanent shelters. Without a doubt many of these would have been caves but whatever form the living quarters took, having an assured supply of food was a major step on the road to civilization. Not having to spend every waking hour trying to hunt food and to avoid becoming food themselves was a big change in the history of early man.

There have been numerous archaeological finds of shells in the remains of primitive man. Many of the shells have had holes drilled in them so that they could be threaded onto cords and worn as ornaments, or simply carried by the owner. This clearly shows that shells were objects of interest to humans even then, but we don't know what role they played. They could have been used as some form of currency, or they may have had ceremonial significance. Then again, they may have simply been for decorative purposes. It is interesting that some shells have been found a very long way from where they originated, which suggests that even this early in history, they were held to have value for trade.

Once a mollusk was found, and its contents consumed, it is not a very big step to imagine that pretty quickly a use was found for the empty shell. Perhaps in the beginning it was just to hold drinking water — I'm sure that empty shells left out in the rain were soon made use of as a source of fresh water. Once the concept of the shell being more than a food casing had been realized, I would think it safe to say that new uses came along pretty rapidly.

Perhaps it took a while longer for shells to be broken up and used as a raw material from which to make other things, but I suspect not. It wouldn't take a vast leap of imagination to use a mussel shell, for instance, as a scraper to clean the fat off animal skins. Once you've got used to this, it wouldn't take much more to sharpen the edges of the shell in order to cut the skin. As soon as you have this understood, you have the basis for all sorts of weapons, such as knives, arrowheads, spears, and so on. Maybe it was not as good as flint, but it would have been much easier to work, and therefore no doubt had its place in the repertoire of prehistoric man's useful objects.

The next step would have been to carry around these useful tools, whereupon they were bound to have become status symbols. Displaying them prominently could well have been the foundation of jewelry — we

know from excavations that in the Mediterranean and the Middle East shells were being used for personal adornment more than thirty thousand years ago. Once mankind was at this stage, it would have been a clear run through to historic times.

The precise purpose and chronology of prehistoric man's use of shells is lost in the mists of time, so we have very little to go on except the odd remnant here and there. The exception to this is where shells have been left in piles after the contents were consumed — sometimes the heaps that have been discovered have been very large indeed. The first historical evidence of shells in human society is from the Minoan and Egyptian civilizations, where they were used for decoration, jewelry, and religious purposes. The Minoans were seafarers, so they used all sorts of maritime images to decorate everything from tombs to everyday utensils — these included shells, octopuses, and mermaids.

The ancient Greeks were very keen on using almost every plant or animal in their art, and shells were no exception. Probably the best known of these is the legend of Aphrodite, the Goddess of Desire, who is said to have risen naked from a scallop shell, and stepped forth through the foaming waves onto the shores of the island of Cythera. A religious cult arose to worship her, and those who did so used shells extensively in the temples they built in her honor.

Shells had many other influences in the eastern Mediterranean where modern civilization is said to have had its birth. For example, Archimedes of Syracuse (287–212 BC), one of the greatest intellects of all time, invented many mechanisms and physical principles that amazed the populace. One of these was what we refer to these days as the "Archimedean Screw," the helix form of screw threads. It is said he invented it while in Egypt, in order to pump out a dry dock for a massive war galley built for pharaoh Ptolemaios IV Philopator. This pump was a rotating helical device that raised water as it was turned, and it is thought that Archimedes' inspiration came from the shape of the turret shell.

No mention of the relationship between ancient Greece and shells would be complete without mentioning the "Golden Fleece." The legend is typical of those of ancient Greece, being a story of deceit, tragedy, and heroic exploit. It concerned King Athamas of Boeotia, who had two children, Phrixus and Helle. These children were the product of his first marriage, and after the death of their mother, he remarried. The children then represented a threat to the future of his second wife, Ino, so she plotted to get rid of them. To cut a long story short, she infected the crops with a disease, and managed to convince the local priests that the gods had deemed the children should be sacrificed at the top of a nearby mountain, in order to save the nation from starvation.

Nephele, the late mother of the children, was meanwhile watching

**Shells for sale in Kenya.**

the goings on from heaven, where she managed to persuade the gods to send a winged golden ram to rescue them from their imminent sacrifice. The children were carried away on its back at the last minute, and it flew off towards the Black Sea, where sadly Helle lost her grip and fell into the sea (now known as the Dardanelles). When he landed, Phrixus sacrificed the ram in gratitude to the gods (some gratitude!), and presented its golden fleece to King Aeetes of Colchis, who was the tyrannical ruler of the land. The king was so pleased with such a treasure that he gave Phrixus his daughter's hand in marriage!

The golden fleece had such value that the king decided the only way to keep it safe was to have it guarded by a dragon, which patroled around it continuously. At this point Jason enters the story — he was the rightful heir to the kingdom of Iolcus in Thessaly, but his throne had been stolen by Pelias, Phrixus' cousin. In order to try and rid himself of Jason's presence, Pelias agreed to hand over the throne, if he was man enough to bring back the golden fleece — a task thought to be suicidal.

Jason then went to fulfil his challenge on the *Argo*, together with somewhere between forty-five and fifty-five men (and possibly one woman). The crew thus immortalized themselves in history as the "Argonauts." Jason was, of course, successful in his mission, and eventually got his throne back.

While all this is very interesting, it may not seem to be relevant to the issue of shells, but in fact they are very much to the fore of this legend, because the golden fleece was almost certainly based on the cloth of gold, a material so far beyond the comprehension of the people of the time, it is not surprising that it found its way into the local mythology. This cloth was made from yarn spun from the "byssal threads" of the Noble Pen shell (*Pinna nobilis*). These are filaments some shells use to attach themselves to the seabed — in this particular species they are a fabulous metallic gold color.

The garments made from cloth of gold were so sheer and fine that they quickly became considered the height of luxury. The "byssal silks" were, however, so difficult to produce that anything made from them commanded prices that could only be met by royalty — they were worn by the kings and queens of Europe throughout history, right up to Queen Victoria, who had a pair of stockings made from them.

The connection between shells and the grandeur of Greece and Rome is nowhere more closely bound than with the story of cloth-dye. In classical times, one of the most valuable of all goods was purple cloth — that is, apart from the "cloth of gold" detailed above. It was used for all manner of things, from carpets to togas, all of which could only be afforded by the fabulously wealthy. The story of how the dye was produced started with the Egyptians and Cretans, who had discovered somewhere around 1500 BC that colors could be obtained from certain shells, but they couldn't work out how to make them permanent. This secret was uncovered by the occupants of a Phoenician town, called Tyre (in present day Lebanon) — they kept the process to themselves, the dye became known as Tyrian Purple, and they got very rich as a result!

We can find examples of the use of Tyrian Purple in many places in Greek legend, such as when Agamemnon returned from Troy (after ten years away). Just before he was murdered by his wife with repeated blows of an axe, he walked into his palace over purple carpets. This was mentioned to signify that even though he had been away for so long, things were still prosperous enough in his absence for his wife to be able to use material of such value for mere carpets.

The dye was extracted by collecting certain shells in the gastropod family — mostly *Murex trunculus*, *Murex brandaris*, and *Thais haemostoma*. These are carnivorous mollusks, which often attack oysters, among others. Each shell would yield only one or two drops of the precious dye, and tens of thousands were needed to color a single garment; many millions were used to make commercially profitable quantities of cloth. The remains of the discarded shells can still be seen in many places to this day!

The shells were mostly caught in special traps that were baited with cockles. Once enough had been obtained to start collecting the dye, the shells were broken open, and the dye-producing gland was removed. Those shells which were too small for this to be practicable were boiled in vast vats, until the valuable dye could be separated. The most prized cloth was that which turned out a deep reddish purple — presumably this was produced by the first batch to be put through the dye, with subsequent batches becoming paler and paler, until it was no longer effective. The Tyrians grew tremendously wealthy from their trade in the dyed cloth, and prospered until the Emperor Nero declared that only he could wear purple, which killed the industry stone dead overnight. It had been going for over a thousand years at this point, so overall they did very well out of it!

The Phoenicians did not restrict their shell-hunting to the Mediterranean. The potential rewards for finding any new sources from which to make dye were so substantial that they went to great lengths to explore new shores. As a nation of experienced seafarers, this was the natural solution to the problem of the diminishing numbers of murex shells.

One of the places they visited was the British Isles, where they found they could obtain large stocks of the Dog Whelk (*Nucella lapillus*), from which they were able to produce a low grade dye. This dye continued to be made from the whelk for centuries after the Phoenicians had left, being used for various tasks, including the manufacture of inks, paints, and of course dyes. These were used through the Dark Ages, and well into Medieval times.

Shells started to become significant in a new domain — that of the military, when heraldic symbols became commonplace on the battlefield, during the 12th and 13th centuries. Whether or not the heraldic devices already existed, we don't know, but as knights began to wear more and more armor it became vitally important to be able to identify them, so they started to carry shields emblazoned with the family coat of arms. Some heraldic shields carried depictions of lions, others of eagles, but about a quarter of them had shells of some description in their make-up. The scallop was particularly popular, and often had religious importance, signifying the wearer had made a pilgrimage to the shrine of St James at Compostella in Spain, or a military excursion to the Holy Wars.

The use of scallops was also very popular during the Renaissance, when they were used in all manner of situations, especially in architectural designs and paintings. The most famous use of a scallop in art is of course, the Birth of Venus, by Botticelli, where she rises from the sea on a large white scallop. Shells have continued to be a common theme in artwork of every kind to this day. The Rococo period used them extensively in porcelain, and on the European continent there was a craze for mounting shells extravagantly in gold or silver, especially in Germany and Austria.

Modern-day shell collecting became established in the late 17th and early 18th centuries, when explorers brought back various artifacts from distant lands. Shells were particularly popular because they traveled well and looked attractive in the cabinets of curios that fashionable wealthy gentlemen put together. They also had a use that many other curios from foreign lands did not, and that was their inclusion in architectural constructions.

This was a time when romanticism was still fashionable, and the fact the Romans liked building grottoes was excuse enough for most of the "big" houses of Europe to build them. It was also a time of "follies" — these were designed to show off the wealth and splendor of the originators. Some were designed to mimic ancient ruins, whereas others were built as towers or temples. Nearly every one of them made use of shells in their construction somewhere: some made use of them everywhere, being almost totally encrusted with shells of one sort or another.

Over the course of the 19th century, collecting went through a transition from an idle pastime of the rich, to an obsessive mania practiced by a class of people who were becoming more and more educated as time went by. This resulted in science becoming the central pivot around which these collections were based. Hence conchology began; this literally means "the study of the shell," whereas these days you will hear the

**Seashells have been used by mankind since the very earliest days for all sorts of uses. Here a common shell is being used as an ocarina — a primitive musical instrument made with only the addition of a few small holes. Many such items have been found by archaeologists; some were made from seashells, others from pieces of bone — the oldest of these date back tens of thousands of years.**

**This conch shell is a spectacular species which is often used to make things like lamp holders. Most shell collectors go pale when they see this done, as they consider it to be vandalism.**

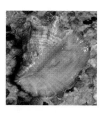

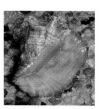

term "malacology." This refers to the study of the shell and the animal within it, in other words the biology of the shell as an organism.

While shells have had their place in western society, in many other cultures they have had huge importance, acting as currency, religious talismans, and fertility symbols. One of the best known forms of shell currency is the Money Cowry (*Cypraea moneta*), although it is only one of 180 species of cowry that was used for this purpose (and thus called the money cowry). Where the cowry occurred naturally, it had a low value, but this increased the further it was taken from its source. At one time huge fortunes were made by Europeans trading cowries for gold, silver, slaves, and other merchandise, between the Pacific and the west coast of Africa.

The tusk shell (*Dentalium pretiosum*) was used as currency by the Indian tribes of the Pacific northwest, whereas in California they used pieces of abalone shells instead. Further down the continent in South America, all the major civilizations used shells in their artwork, often in a manner similar to that of the early Greeks — yet another suggestion that there was communication between the two continents at that time.

The cultures of the Pacific islanders were probably more bound up with shells than any other — this is not surprising when you consider their proximity to the sea and the fantastic range of shells at their disposal. They used shells for everything possible, from headpieces to balers to keep down the water level in their canoes. Personal adornments made from shells are common in almost every culture across the world, but the vast array to choose from in the warm Pacific waters made the others produced there the most extravagant.

Large shells, particularly tritons, chanks, helmets, and conches have been used by primitive cultures as trumpets or horns since the earliest civilizations began. Sometimes they were to call together men for war, in other places they were just to call the cattle in! To convert a shell into something suitable for a horn was simplicity itself — a hole was made somewhere near the apex. This is something that does not amuse shell collectors, but it is at least better than turning them into holders for electric light bulbs!

The list of uses for shells is almost endless — for instance, some primitive peoples discovered that they could use auger shells as simple drills to pierce a variety of natural materials. Other tribes fashioned fish hooks out of parts of various types of shells, shaping them differently depending on their intended catch. In the south Pacific men shaved their beards with specially sharpened fragments of shells, which also served to cut and clean fish, skin animals

The following pages give a sample selection of the types of shell available to the collector.

# The Shells
# Class Bivalvia

| | |
|---|---|
| **Common name:** | Pacific Thorny Oyster |
| **Scientific name:** | *Spondylus princeps* |
| **Descriptor:** | Broderip |
| **Superfamily:** | Pectinacea |
| **Family:** | Spondylidae |
| **Distribution:** | Gulf of California, southward |
| **Size:** | 3-6in (75-150mm) |

The Pacific Thorny Oyster is one of a group that is referred to as either "Thorny Oysters" or as "Chrysanthemum Shells." There are about a hundred different species, most of which cement themselves to rock and coral in the sub-tidal zone. These exquisite shells are rarely found in perfect condition as their spines are easily damaged in their turbulent habitat. The spines' purpose is twofold — they help to keep predatory mollusks at bay and they also support large numbers of algae and sponges, which give them excellent camouflage.

**Common name:** Regal Thorny Oyster

**Scientific name:** *Spondylus regius*

**Descriptor:** Linnaeus, 1758

**Superfamily:** Pectinacea

**Family:** Spondylidae

**Distribution:** Japan and southeast Asia

**Size:** 5-8in (150-200mm)

The Regal Thorny Oyster lives in deeper water than many others in the family, but it too uses its spines in the same manner — that is for protection and concealment. This species, along with most of the other thorny oysters, is very popular with collectors as it has such a fine looking shell. In many cultures the shells had important religious or ceremonial significance.

| | |
|---|---|
| **Common name:** | Fluted or Scaly Giant Clam |
| **Scientific name:** | *Tridacna squamosa* |
| **Descriptor:** | Lamarck, 1819 |
| **Family:** | Tridacnidae |
| **Genus:** | Tridacna |
| **Distribution:** | Indo-Pacific |
| **Size:** | 24in (600mm) |

The Tridacnidae family consists of giant clams — there are seven species in the Tridacna genus, and two in the Hippopus genus. They all come from the Indo-Pacific region, where they are considered endangered — although fortunately they are now protected by the C.I.T.E.S. treaty. Modern techniques for culturing these clams are, however, helping to restore the balance. In the western Pacific, on the islands of the Solomons and Palau, there are several marine farms where large numbers are being successfully grown — these are then mainly used to supply commercial aquaria, but also for restocking reefs . There are many fascinating aspects to the giant clams — some, such as *Tridacna gigas* can grow to enormous sizes, exceeding 5ft (1.5m) in length and 550lb (250kg) in weight. One of their other unusual features is that they are the only mollusks which have established symbiotic relationships with zooxanthellae algae. They have evolved to incorporate these primitive plants internally: the algae then uses sunlight to generate food for the clam. In doing so the algae produce incredible colors in the mantle, especially in *Tridacna crocea*. This is beneficial to both partners in the relationship: the clams get food, and the algae get a place to live. While the clams offer a much safer environment for the algae than most other marine habitats, they have a surprising number of predators. Among mollusks these include "rice" snails (Pyramidellidae) which attack the mantle, and murex shells which bore through the shell and eat the clam from the inside. Many fish such as wrasses, angels, and blennies may also attack the mantle, and crabs, certain shrimps, and predatory worms also take their toll. There are many other threats to these wonderful creatures — they are sensitive to heavy metal poisoning from pollutants, as well as excessive phosphate or iodine levels. Their internal algae's reliance on the sun also makes the giant clams dependant on high light levels, which limits them to shallow waters. When you consider all these predators, threats, and specific requirements, it's a surprise that they manage to survive at all! The Fluted or Scaly Giant Clam is a welcome addition to most shell collections as it is so unusually constructed. This and its large size — about 2ft (600mm) — makes it stand out in a display case. When alive their mantles are impressively colored with various shades of blue, green, yellow, and orange arranged in spots and bands, something that makes them popular in marine aquaria

| Common name: | Elongate Giant Clam |
|---|---|
| Scientific name: | *Tridacna maxima* |
| Descriptor: | Roding, 1798 |
| Family: | Tridacnidae |
| Genus: | Tridacna |
| Distribution: | East Africa to Polynesia |
| Size: | Up to 16in (400mm) |

The Elongate Giant Clam is another member of this small family of big-shelled mollusks which has beautifully colored mantles — in this species they are mostly green and blue. Those species of giant clams which are highly colored are the ones which live close to the surface so that their internal colonies of algae can receive enough sunlight to prosper, and in doing so provide the clam with various nutrients.

| Scientific name: | *Tridacna crocea* |
| --- | --- |
| Family: | Tridacnidae |
| Genus: | Tridacna |
| Distribution: | Indo-Pacific |
| Size: | 9in (230mm) |

The mantle of a living *Tridacna crocea* makes it one of the most beautifully colored of all mollusks — this makes it a popular choice for exotic marine aquaria, especially as they are the smallest of the giant clams. In such conditions they may live for up to 10 years. They have special algae in their body tissues which are energy-producing — these use sunlight as fuel, which in turn means that the clam must live near the surface. They are usually found in large colonies, where they often burrow into coral and soft rocks. This is achieved by the secretion of acids to soften the material they are trying to work their way into — they then use their shells to grind their way in mechanically.

| Common name: | Bear's Paw or Horseshoe Clam |
|---|---|
| Scientific name: | *Hippopus hippopus* |
| Descriptor: | Linnaeus, 1758 |
| Family: | Tridacnidae |
| Genus: | Hippopus |
| Distribution: | Pacific. |
| Size: | 16in (400mm) |

The Bear's Paw or Horseshoe Clam is a common species of the warmer Pacific regions, where it can be found down to depths of about 20ft (6m), usually on sandy bottoms near coral reefs. It has a heavily constructed shell, which reaches sizes of 16in (400mm) as an adult.

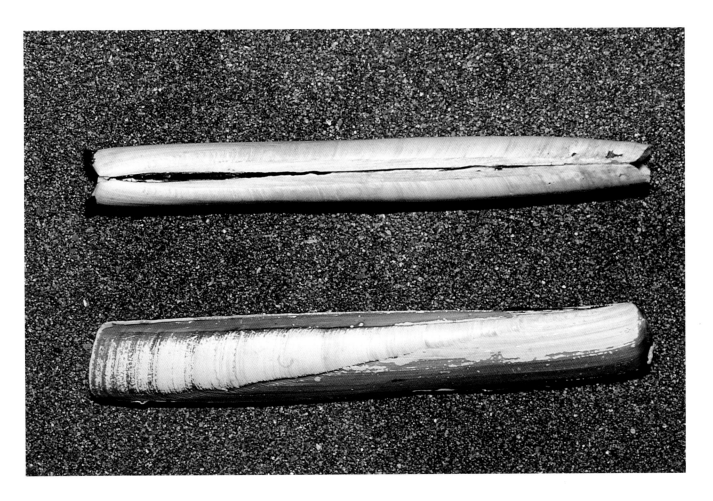

| | |
|---|---|
| **Common name:** | Razor shell |
| **Scientific name:** | *Ensis arcuatus* |
| **Family:** | Solenidae |
| **Distribution:** | Northern Norway to the Mediterranean |
| **Size:** | 7in (180mm) |

The various species of razor shells live vertically in sand, using a muscular foot that enables them to burrow faster than a man can dig. They inhabit the inter-tidal zone down to about 100ft (30m). They are edible, and where they are plentiful they are often collected for consumption. The widespread effects of pollution and over-collecting have drastically reduced the numbers of these mollusks in many areas.

| Common name: | Virgate Tellin |
|---|---|
| Scientific name: | *Tellina virgata* |
| Descriptor: | Linnaeus, 1758 |
| Family: | Tellinidae |
| Distribution: | Indo-Pacific |
| Size: | 2.5in (65mm) |

The Virgate Tellin is one of a group of about 200 mollusks that posses thin, flat shells which often have brightly colored markings. They live in sandy areas in tropical and warm temperate regions, where they burrow very quickly and deeply. This species is common in the shallow waters of the Indian and Pacific Oceans.

| Common name: | Catrina Scallop |
|---|---|
| Scientific name: | *Argopecten circularis* |
| Descriptor: | Sowerby, 1835 |
| Family: | Pectinidae |
| Distribution: | Pacific coast of Mexico and California |
| Size: | 2-3in (50-75mm) |

The Catrina Scallop is one of the most impressively marked of its family. It is of more than visual interest, however, as it is farmed commercially in large beds at depths of up to 100ft (30m). The financial significance of this species makes it the subject of scientific research, which is a welcome source of extra knowledge about shells and their environment.

| Common name: | Australian Scallop |
|---|---|
| Scientific name: | *Chlamys australis* |
| Descriptor: | Sowerby, 1847 |
| Family: | Pectinidae |
| Distribution: | Australia |
| Size: | 3-4in (75-100mm) |

The Australian Scallop is one of several hundred scallop species that occur worldwide, many of which have commercial importance where there are fished for human consumption. The two halves of the shell are known as "valves" — the left one is usually the lower of the two, and is usually more convex. This one is very variable as can be seen from the range of colors shown here.

| Common name: | Swift's Scallop |
|---|---|
| Scientific name: | *Chlamys swifti* |
| Descriptor: | Bernardi |
| Family: | Pectinidae |
| Distribution: | Japan |
| Size: | 3-5in (75-125mm) |

The Swift's Scallop is a deep water species from the waters around Japan. Like the other members of the scallop family, it moves around in a curious "flapping" manner — it sucks in water, and then snaps the two halves of its shell together, which creates a jet that causes it to move in the opposite direction. The sight of groups of these mollusks swimming together is quite amazing!

| Common name: | Giant Cockle |
|---|---|
| Scientific name: | *Plagiocardium pseudolima* |
| Descriptor: | Lamarck |
| Family: | Cardiidae |
| Distribution: | Cockles can be found all in all waters of the world |
| Size: | 4in (100mm) |

The Giant Cockle is — as its name suggests — a very large species of this extensive family. Its very pronounced ribs and vivid coloration make it an excellent addition to the bivalve section of any shell collection.

# Class Cephalopoda

| Common name: | Pearly or Chambered Nautilus |
| --- | --- |
| Scientific name: | *Nautilus pompilius* |
| Descriptor: | Linnaeus, 1758 |
| Family: | Nautiloidea |
| Distribution: | Indian and southwestern Pacific Oceans |
| Size: | 6-8in (200mm) |

The Pearly or Chambered Nautilus is an amazing creature that belongs to the same class as the octopus, squid, and cuttlefish. It is common in the warmer waters of the Indian and Pacific Oceans, where it is a free-swimmer, living at depths of between 160ft and 330ft (50-100m) — it does, however, rise toward the surface at night.

| Scientific name: | *Murex negrispinosus* |
|---|---|
| Descriptor: | Reeve, 1845 |
| Superfamily: | Muricacea |
| Family: | Muricidae |
| Distribution: | Indo-Pacific |
| Size: | 4in (100mm) |

There are something like a thousand different species of Murex shells, which makes them one of the more extensive families of mollusks. Their intricate shapes and structures make them very popular with shell collectors, who often also find their habits very interesting. The various members of this fascinating family are carnivorous, preying on other mollusks throughout the tropical and warmer temperate seas of the world. Their mode of attack is to gain a foothold on their victim's shell, and then to bore a hole through it using the radula as a drill — this is made easier by the use of some powerful digestive acids. In some places they can be a serious pest — for example where oysters are farmed commercially. Most Murex shells have strong spines or fronds which probably act as in defense as well as a framework on which seaweed and other marine plants can grow — this creates a very effective camouflage. There are, however, many different habitats in which Murex shells can be found — some are dwellers in muddy situations, some like sandy bottoms, whereas others prefer to live on coral reefs. *Murex negrispinosus* is one of the more uncommon species of Murex shells — it lives in shallow water amongst the sea-grass on muddy bottoms. The spines are particularly impressive, which must deter many predators, although it makes them more attractive to collectors.

| Common name: | Purple Dye Murex |
|---|---|
| Scientific name: | *Bolinus brandaris* |
| Descriptor: | Linnaeus, 1758 |
| Superfamily: | Muricacea |
| Family: | Muricidae |
| Distribution: | Mediterranean, North Africa |
| Size: | 3.5in (90mm) |

The Purple Dye Murex was highly prized by many early Mediterranean civilizations as the source of the purple dye used in the production of the high quality cloths from which robes were made for the rich and powerful. Entire cities depended on these shells for their prosperity.

| Common name: | Regal Murex |
|---|---|
| Scientific name: | *Hexaplex regius* |
| Descriptor: | Swainson, 1821 |
| Superfamily: | Muricacea |
| Family: | Muricidae |
| Distribution: | West Mexico to Peru |
| Size: | 6in (150mm) |

The Regal Murex is yet another example of just how varied the shells of this family can be. It is a heavily built species, and has shorter, stouter, spines than most of the others. When it is covered with seaweed, it is almost invisible to all but the closest inspection.

| Common name: | Rose-Branch Murex |
|---|---|
| Scientific name: | *Chicoreus palmarosae* |
| Descriptor: | Lamarck, 1822 |
| Superfamily: | Muricacea |
| Family: | Muricidae |
| Distribution: | Indo-Pacific |
| Size: | 3-5in (75-125mm) |

The Rose-Branch Murex is a common species, but this does not detract from the beauty of its exquisite fronds and coloration. It can be found throughout the warmer waters of the Indian and Pacific Oceans, at depths between 6ft and 60ft (2-18m).

| Common name: | Mancinella Rock Shell |
|---|---|
| Scientific name: | *Thais (Stramonita) mancinella* |
| Descriptor: | Linnaeus, 1758 |
| Superfamily: | Muricacea |
| Family: | Thaididae |
| Distribution: | Southwest Pacific |
| Size: | 2in (50mm) |

The "Rock" shells, as this family are usually known, are heavily constructed species, which live in large colonies and prey on various shallow water mollusks, such as mussels and oysters. This can make them a serious problem for commercial fisheries. The Mancinella Rock Shell is one of the smaller species, and only grows to about 2in (50mm) in length. It can be found in the southwestern Pacific and into the Indian Ocean.

Common name: Mawe's Latiaxis

Scientific name: *Latiaxis mawae*

Descriptor: Griffith and Pidgeon, 1834

Superfamily: Muricacea

Family: Coralliophylidae

Distribution: Japan to Australia

Size: 2.5in (60mm)

These mollusks are usually known as "Latiaxis" shells, some of which were once highly prized by early collectors. There are not many Latiaxis species and most live near, or on, coral or various other coelenterates. It seems that they feed by sucking out the body fluids of these organisms — they have no radula, so they cannot bore their way into shelled animals as other mollusks, such as the Murex shells. The Mawe's Latiaxis was first found in the early 1800s, when it commanded very high prices amongst the fanatical collectors of the time. It has since been found in larger numbers, but as it is a deep water species, it is never going to be available to every modern-day enthusiast.

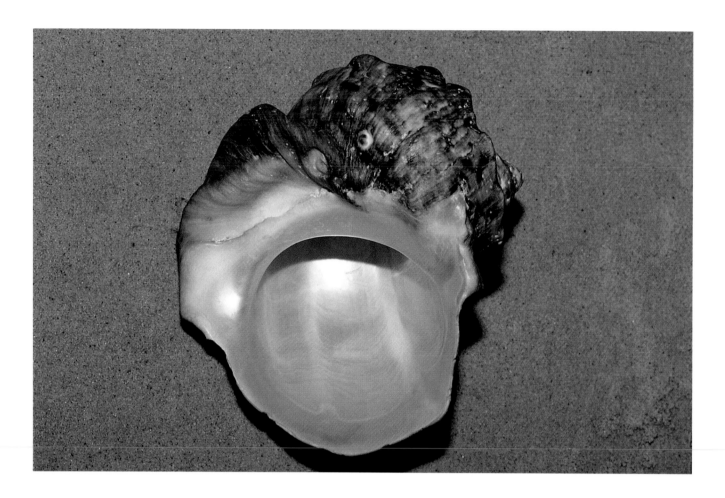

| Common name: | Great Green Turban |
|---|---|
| Scientific name: | *Turbo (Taeniaturbo) marmoratus* |
| Descriptor: | Linnaeus, 1758 |
| Superfamily: | Trochacea |
| Family: | Turbinidae |
| Distribution: | Indo-Pacific. |
| Size: | 8in (200mm) |

The turban shells are generally a heavily built conical shape, with a similarly solid operculum. They are mostly found in shallow water, where they feed on vegetative matter, such as seaweed and algae. The Great Green Turban is the largest of the Turbinidae family, and has a solid, heavy shell. It is the original source of mother of pearl, and as such still has a significant commercial value for use in jewelry.

| Common name: | Delphinula Snail |
| --- | --- |
| Scientific name: | *Angaria delphinula* |
| Descriptor: | Linnaeus, 1758 |
| Superfamily: | Trochacea |
| Family: | Trochidae |
| Distribution: | Indo-Pacific |
| Size: | 3in (75mm) |

The Trochidae family is composed of the top shells. The many hundreds of species have an enormous distribution, occurring in shallow water throughout the tropical and temperate waters of the world. They are often found in large groups, among the seaweed and rocks they inhabit, where they graze on vegetative material. Some species are collected commercially for human consumption, although many are too small to be worth the effort. If a top shell is dislodged from its resting place it will retreat behind a round, horny operculum, where it will stay until it has decided that the threat has gone. The Delphinula Snail is one of the bigger species in the Trochidae; combined with its solid shell this gives it quite a heavy construction. It has a brown, horny, operculum and its availability is very variable.

| Common name: | Commercial Top |
|---|---|
| Scientific name: | *Tectus (Rochia) niloticus* |
| Descriptor: | Linnaeus, 1767 |
| Superfamily: | Trochacea |
| Family: | Trochidae |
| Distribution: | Indo-Pacific |
| Size: | Up to 6in (150mm) high |

The Commercial Top is so called because it has been used for years — probably thousands of years — as a source of material from which to make various small objects. These days the shells are still used for this purpose, with the better known products being things like buttons. Fortunately, it is a common species, so this human activity is unlikely to have a serious impact on its survival as a species.

**Common name:** American or Noble Sundial

**Scientific name:** *Architectonica nobilis*

**Descriptor:** Roding, 1798

**Superfamily:** Architectonicacea

**Family:** Architectonicidae

**Distribution:** Central America

**Size:** 2in (50mm)

The Architectonicacea are the Sundial shells, of which there are about 40 or so species. They are only found in areas with warm water, so they are mostly restricted to the shallow waters of the tropical and sub-tropical areas of the world. There are a few deep-water species, but they are quite rare, and so are highly prized. The American or Noble Sundial is sometimes also known as the Common Atlantic Sundial. It is common wherever there is a sandy bottom in shallow waters through-out most of its range.

| Common name: | Common Harp |
|---|---|
| Scientific name: | *Harpa harpa* |
| Descriptor: | Linnaeus, 1758 |
| Superfamily: | Volutacea |
| Family: | Harpidae |
| Distribution: | Indo-Pacific. |
| Size: | 2-3in (50-75mm) |

The Common Harp is a member of a small family of 14 or so species, which are confined to tropical waters. Most of them have very attractive shells which are finely sculpted, with strong axial ribs. They are rapid carnivorous mollusks which burrow in sand in pursuit of their prey. In order to do so, they have a broad foot which in an emergency they can self-amputate in order to escape from predators — this is known as "autotomy."

| Common name: | Imperial Volute |
|---|---|
| Scientific name: | *Cymbiola imperialis robinsona* |
| Descriptor: | Burch, 1954 |
| Superfamily: | Volutacea |
| Family: | Volutidae |
| Distribution: | Philippines and surrounding areas |
| Size: | 10in (250mm) |

The Volutidae is an extensive and very interesting family, with over 200 species of predatory volutes. They have a distribution that includes almost all the seas of the world. By far the majority are found in warm waters, but there are some species which can be found in the colder waters of the temperate regions — there are, however, even a few which inhabit Antarctic areas. They are mostly burrowers in sand, where they use their ability to move fast to catch up with their prey and devour it. The Imperial Volute, like many shells, occurs in more than one form — this one is the subspecies "robinsona," which lacks the spiral markings of the typical form. There are many other variations on the "type" species, some of which are different enough to be given names of their own, while others are not. It has a heavy shell which when fully grown is a substantial construction.

| Common name: | Princely or Courtier Volute |
|---|---|
| Scientific name: | *Cymbiola aulica* |
| Descriptor: | Sowerby 1825 |
| Superfamily: | Volutacea |
| Family: | Volutidae |
| Distribution: | Philippines. |
| Size: | 6in (150mm). |

The Princely or Courtier Volute is an uncommon species with a solid shell. The photograph shows what is known as "crabbing" — this is where the shell has been damaged at some stage in its lifetime, and has subsequently been repaired.

Common name: Heavy Baler Shell
Scientific name: *Melo umbilicatus*
Descriptor: Sowerby, 1826
Superfamily: Volutacea
Family: Volutidae
Distribution: Northern and eastern coasts of Australia
Size: 16in (400mm)

The Heavy Baler Shell of the northern and eastern coasts of Australia is
well known to the native peoples who have been using them to bale
out water from their boats since the areas were first populated —
hence the name!

| Common name: | Elephant's Snout |
|---|---|
| Scientific name: | *Cymbian glans* |
| Descriptor: | Gmelin, 1791 |
| Superfamily: | Volutacea |
| Family: | Volutidae |
| Distribution: | West Africa |
| Size: | 12in (300mm) |

The Elephant's Snout shells pictured were found in the Gambia, although the species occurs along most of the coasts of western Africa. These specimens were purchased from local fishermen who were only too happy to supplement their income with tourist money!

| Common name: | Elliot's Volute |
|---|---|
| Scientific name: | *Amoria ellioti* |
| Descriptor: | Sowerby, 1864 |
| Superfamily: | Volutacea |
| Family: | Volutidae |
| Distribution: | South and west Australia |
| Size: | 3-4.5in (75-110mm) |

The Elliot's Volute is a well marked species with a strong shell. Like the other members of the Volutidae, it is carnivorous, using speed and agility to overhaul and devour its prey.

| Common name: | Bat Volute |
|---|---|
| Scientific name: | *Cymbiola vespertilio* |
| Descriptor: | Linnaeus, 1758 |
| Superfamily: | Volutacea |
| Family: | Volutidae |
| Distribution: | Indo-Pacific. |
| Size: | 2-4.5in (50-115mm) |

The Bat Volute is a common species in the Indian and Pacific Oceans, where it is very variable in coloration and markings. This variability extends to the direction of its coils — most are right-handed or "dextral,", but "sinistral" — that is left-handed specimens — are more common than with most other volutes.

| | |
|---|---|
| **Common name:** | Abyssal Volute |
| **Scientific name:** | *Volutocorbis abyssicola* |
| **Descriptor:** | Adams and Reeve, 1848 |
| **Superfamily:** | Volutacea |
| **Family:** | Volutidae |
| **Distribution:** | South Africa. |
| **Size:** | 3-4 inches (75-100mm). |

The Abyssal Volute is a deep-water species which is one of the reasons that it is not very colorful — as you go down in depth, there is less and less light, and so colors become less visible. The first of these to be filtered out is red, and the rest follow soon after. Consequently, there is no reason for abyssal mollusks to develop the exquisite markings and colors of species that live nearer the surface.

| Common name: | Episcopal Miter |
| --- | --- |
| Scientific name: | *Mitra mitra* |
| Descriptor: | Linnaeus, 1758 |
| Superfamily: | Volutacea |
| Family: | Mitridae |
| Distribution: | Indo-Pacific |
| Size: | 6in (150mm) |

A family of ten genera and many species, the Miters live in sand, coral and seaweed in intertidal and shallow areas. Carnivorous, they are scavengers of tropical and temperate seas. With its distinctive markings, the Episcopal Miter is probably the best known of the Miters — it is also the largest. It is quite similar to the Papal Miter, but is not as stout. They occur throughout the Indian and Pacific Oceans, where they live as carnivores on sandy bottoms.

| | |
|---|---|
| **Common name:** | Queen Miter |
| **Scientific name:** | *Vexillum regina* |
| **Descriptor:** | Sowerby, 1828 |
| **Superfamily:** | Volutacea |
| **Family:** | Mitridae |
| **Distribution:** | Indo-Pacific |
| **Size:** | 2-3in (50-75mm) |

The Queen Miter is easily confused with other similarly marked species. It inhabits the Indian and Pacific regions, where it lives in sand amongst rocks and coral. It can be found at depths anywhere between 15ft and 100ft (4.5-30m).

| | |
|---|---|
| **Common name:** | Tent Olive |
| **Scientific name:** | *Oliva porphyria* |
| **Descriptor:** | Linnaeus, 1758 |
| **Superfamily:** | Volutacea |
| **Family:** | Olividae |
| **Distribution:** | Gulf of California, Panama |
| **Size:** | 3-4.5in (80-110mm) |

The Tent Olive is the largest of its family, and has beautiful markings, which made it particularly highly prized when it was first brought back to Europe by explorers returning from the Panamanian coasts.

| | |
|---|---|
| **Common name:** | Red-Mouthed or Pacific Olive |
| **Scientific name:** | *Oliva miniacea* |
| **Descriptor:** | Roding, 1798 |
| **Superfamily:** | Volutacea |
| **Family:** | Olividae |
| **Distribution:** | Indo-Pacific |
| **Size:** | 3.5in (90mm) |

The Red-Mouthed or Pacific Olive can cause a great deal of confusion, due to being very variable. It has a very heavy and solid shell, and some have exquisite combinations of color and markings.

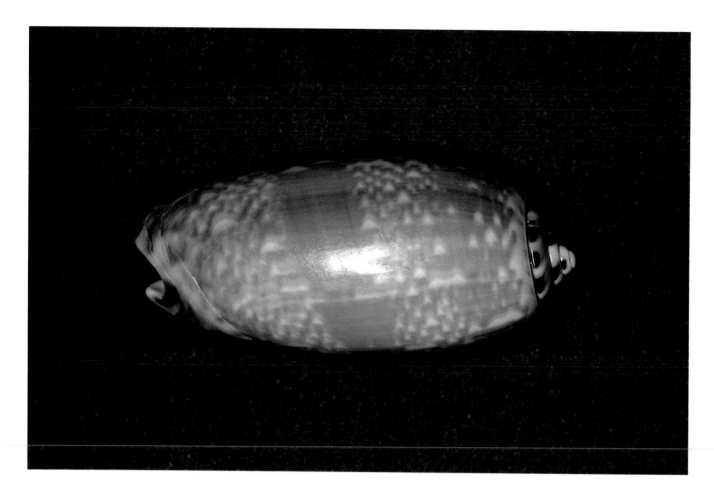

| Common name: | Three Colored Olive |
|---|---|
| Scientific name: | *Oliva tricolor* |
| Descriptor: | Lamarck, 1811 |
| Superfamily: | Volutacea |
| Family: | Olividae |
| Distribution: | Indian Ocean to west Pacific |
| Size: | 2.5in (60mm) |

The Three Colored Olive is usually more easily identified than some of the other species, as it is less variable. It has a heavily built shell and distinctive markings.

| Common name: | Colossal False Fusus |
|---|---|
| Scientific name: | *Hemifusus colosseus* |
| Descriptor: | Lamarck, 1816 |
| Superfamily: | Buccinacea |
| Family: | Melongenidae |
| Distribution: | Japan, Indo-Pacific |

The Melongenidae family consists of the Giant Whelks and conches, which are mostly carnivores or scavengers in shallow waters. Most are quite large, and one — the Australian or False Trumpet (*Syrinx aruanus*) is the biggest gastropod in the world. The Colossal False Fusus is quite a common shell, although it rarely finds its way into shell collections as most of the fishermen who find them cook them in the shell and eat the contents. This destroys the shell, and so it doesn't come onto the market very often. In some areas it is used as a trumpet.

| | |
|---|---|
| **Common name:** | Great Hairy Melongena |
| **Scientific name:** | *Pugilina morio* |
| **Descriptor:** | Linnaeus, 1758 |
| **Superfamily:** | Buccinacea |
| **Family:** | Melongenidae |
| **Distribution:** | Trinidad, Brazil, West Africa |
| **Size:** | 7in (175mm) |

The Great Hairy Melongena shown here was bought from local fishermen in the Gambia, in West Africa. Its rich and dark coloration makes it stand out from the other members of its family, and its well-balanced proportions make it a very presentable member of any collection.

| Common name: | Lightning or Perverse Whelk |
|---|---|
| Scientific name: | *Busycon perversum* |
| Descriptor: | Linnaeus, 1758 |
| Superfamily: | Buccinacea |
| Family: | Melongenidae |
| Distribution: | Florida, West Indies, northeast Mexico |
| Size: | 4-16in (100-375mm) |

The Lightning Whelk is a member of the genus which is sometimes known as the "Fulgur Whelks," of which there are six species. It is unusual in that the shell is normally sinistral — that is with a left-hand spiral; it can, however, be either left or right-handed.

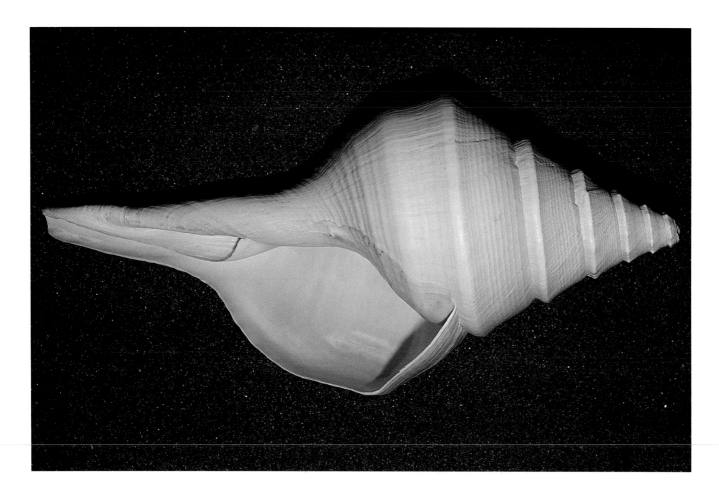

| | |
|---|---|
| **Common name:** | Australian or False Trumpet |
| **Scientific name:** | *Syrinx aruanus* |
| **Descriptor:** | Linnaeus, 1758 |
| **Superfamily:** | Buccinacea |
| **Family:** | Melongenidae |
| **Distribution:** | North Australia |
| **Size:** | 24-36in (600-900mm) |

The Australian or False Trumpet is the largest gastropod in the world, and as such has been used by native peoples for years as a utensil for gathering water. It can grow to 3ft (300mm) in length, which combined with its thick shell makes it very heavy indeed. Large specimens are so prized by collectors that they are endangered in the wild, making them hard to find.

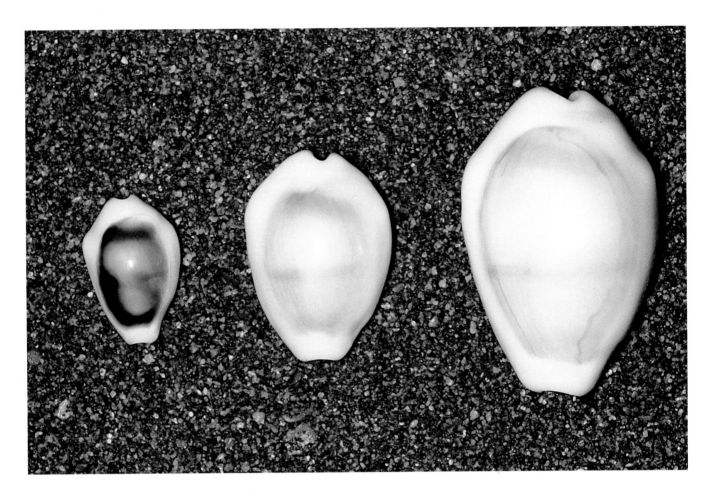

| Common name: | Money Cowry |
|---|---|
| Scientific name: | *Cypraea moneta* |
| Descriptor: | Linnaeus, 1758 |
| Superfamily: | Cypraeacea |
| Family: | Cypraeidae |
| Distribution: | East Africa through Indian Ocean to Hawaii |
| Size: | 1.5in (40mm) |

The Money Cowry is famous for the influence it had on the expansion of European empires throughout the world. This is because it was used as currency by many cultures — at one time two or three good specimens would buy a young wife! As the greedy western traders sought to exploit this source of wealth, they flooded the market, making the Money Cowry close to worthless. The young cowries are very different to the adults, as can be seen from the illustration here. They can also be very variable, which can be very confusing to collectors — ideally a series will be acquired which allows for easier identification when problem specimens are examined.

| Common name: | Sloping Cowry |
|---|---|
| Scientific name: | *Cypraea declivis* |
| Descriptor: | Sowerby, 1870 |
| Superfamily: | Cypraeacea |
| Family: | Cypraeidae |
| Distribution: | South Australia |
| Size: | 1.2in (30mm) |

The Sloping Cowry is a classic example of a species that is markedly different between the juvenile and adult stages. The specimen illustrated here is a juvenile — the adult can be anything from a cream color, through to a rose pink. This range of coloration can be very frustrating when trying to make a positive identification of an indeterminate form.

Common name: Caurica Cowry
Scientific name: *Cypraea caurica*
Descriptor: Linnaeus, 1758
Superfamily: Cypraeacea
Family: Cypraeidae
Distribution: Southeast Africa to Samoa
Size: 2in (50mm)

The Caurica Cowry is usually reasonably easy to identify as it has very pronounced "teeth" as can be seen here. It is common throughout most of its range, which extends from southern Africa to the Pacific. It has several racial forms, some of which are more "tubular" than egg-shaped.

| | |
|---|---|
| **Common name:** | Hump-Back Cowry |
| **Scientific name:** | *Cypraea mauritiana* |
| **Descriptor:** | Linnaeus, 1758 |
| **Superfamily:** | Cypraeacea |
| **Family:** | Cypraeidae |
| **Distribution:** | Indo-Pacific. |
| **Size:** | 3in (75mm). |

The Hump-Back Cowry is another species where the juvenile is very different to the adult, as shown in the sequence above. There are many experienced collectors who have been confused by the juvenile forms as their coloration and markings differ so much that making a positive identification can be very hard. They have very solid shells as they tend to inhabit areas where there is rough water.

Common name: Eyed Cowry
Scientific name: *Cypraea argus*
Descriptor: Linnaeus, 1758
Superfamily: Cypraeacea
Family: Cypraeidae
Distribution: Indo-Pacific
Size: 2-3.5in (50-90mm)

The Eyed Cowry is yet another species from the Indian and Pacific Oceans, although this one is much more uncommon than the others described in this book. Its attractive markings make it very popular with collectors — it is very variable in size, so larger specimens can be comparatively expensive.

| Common name: | Scorpion Conch |
|---|---|
| Scientific name: | *Lambis scorpius* |
| Descriptor: | Linnaeus, 1758 |
| Superfamily: | Strombacea |
| Family: | Strombidae |
| Genus: | Lambis |
| Distribution: | Indian and Pacific Oceans |
| Size: | 3.5-7in (100-180mm) |

The various species of the Strombidae family are divided into the genus Lambis (the spider conches), the genus Strombus (conches), and also the genera Tibia and Terebellum. The Scorpion Conch is an excellent example of the Lambis genus — it is quite unmistakable with its distinctive outline. The males are usually smaller than the females, and are found between 15ft and 60ft (4.5-18m) in depth, in the Indian and Pacific Oceans where they are reasonably common.

| | |
|---|---|
| **Common name:** | Chiragra Spider Conch |
| **Scientific name:** | *Lambis chiragra* |
| **Descriptor:** | Linnaeus, 1758 |
| **Superfamily:** | Strombacea |
| **Family:** | Strombidae |
| **Genus:** | Lambis |
| **Distribution:** | East Indian Ocean to Polynesia |
| **Size:** | Female 10in (250mm), Male 7in (175mm) |

The Chiragra Spider Conch is a good example of the sexual dimorphism that is so common in this genus. The female is much bigger than the male, which was once thought to be an entirely different species, and was accordingly given the separate Latin name of *Lambis rugosa*. It occurs in the southwestern Pacific, where it is quite common.

| Common name: | Laciniate Conch |
|---|---|
| Scientific name: | *Strombus sinuatus* |
| Descriptor: | Humphrey, 1786 |
| Superfamily: | Strombacea |
| Family: | Strombidae |
| Genus: | Strombus |
| Distribution: | Southwest Pacific |
| Size: | 5in (120mm) |

The Laciniate Conch is a shallow-water species, which, in keeping with the other members of the Strombus genus, has a solid shell and a horny operculum which is long and narrow. Another factor common to its close relatives is that it has a powerful muscular foot which enables it to move very fast for a species with such a large and heavy shell. The ability to move so quickly is unusual because they are vegetarians — normally it is only the predatory species that move rapidly.

| Common name: | Lister's Conch |
|---|---|
| Scientific name: | *Strombus listeri* |
| Descriptor: | Gray, 1852 |
| Superfamily: | Strombacea |
| Family: | Strombidae |
| Genus: | Strombus |
| Distribution: | Bay of Bengal, Indian Ocean |
| Size: | 6in (150mm) |

The Lister's Conch is a good illustration of just how little we know about the seabeds of this planet. It was thought to be a rare species until a dredging operation for cable-laying brought up lots of them in the Bay of Bengal.

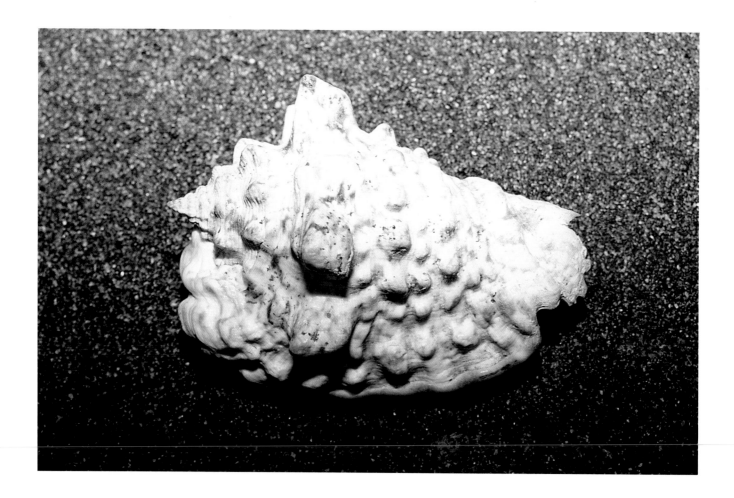

| Common name: | Silver Conch |
|---|---|
| Scientific name: | *Strombus lentiginosus* |
| Descriptor: | Jousseaume, 1886 |
| Superfamily: | Strombacea |
| Family: | Strombidae |
| Genus: | Strombus |
| Distribution: | Tropical Indo-Pacific |
| Size: | 4in (100mm). |

The Silver Conch is typical of the conchs in that it has a particularly solid and heavy shell, which helps to protect it against the large numbers of predators that would be only too happy to include it in their diet. The tropical Indian Ocean where it lives abounds with such animals, including other mollusks, such as the various species of Murex shells.

| Common name: | Wide-Mouth Pacific Conch |
|---|---|
| Scientific name: | *Strombus latissimus* |
| Descriptor: | Linnaeus, 1758 |
| Superfamily: | Strombacea |
| Family: | Strombidae |
| Genus: | Strombus |
| Distribution: | Philippines, West Pacific |
| Size: | 8in (200mm) |

The Wide-Mouth Pacific Conch is another shallow-water species, but this one is remarkable in that it has a very heavy duty shell, even when compared with the other members of this heavily built genus. It is an uncommon species which is usually collected by divers from the sandy bottoms between coral reefs.

| | |
|---|---|
| **Common name:** | Arabian Tibia |
| **Scientific name:** | *Tibia insulae-chorab* |
| **Descriptor:** | Roding, 1798 |
| **Superfamily:** | Strombacea |
| **Family:** | Strombidae |
| **Genus:** | Tibia |
| **Distribution:** | Indo-Pacific from Red Sea to Philippines |
| **Size:** | 6.5in (160mm) |

This species is called the "Arabian" Tibia, which can be misleading, as it not only comes from the Red Sea, but it can also be found as far away as the Philippines! It frequents the sub-tidal habitats, usually preferring muddy bottoms. It occurs in two main forms, "chorab" and "curta" — this one is "chorab."

| Common name: | Red Helmet or Bull's-Mouth Conch |
|---|---|
| Scientific name: | *Cypraecassis rufa* |
| Descriptor: | Linnaeus, 1758 |
| Superfamily: | Tonnacea |
| Family: | Cassididae |
| Distribution: | Indo-Pacific |
| Size: | 4-7in (100-180mm) |

The Red Helmet or Bull's Mouth Conch is a common species in the warmer waters of the Indian and Pacific regions. It can be found at depths of between 10ft and 60ft (3-18m), where they feed on a variety of marine organisms, having a particular liking for sea urchins.

| Common name: | Graceful Fig Shell |
|---|---|
| Scientific name: | *Ficus gracilis* |
| Descriptor: | Sowerby, 1825 |
| Superfamily: | Tonnacea |
| Family: | Ficidae |
| Distribution: | South Japan and east Asia |
| Size: | 6 inches (150mm) |

The Graceful Fig Shell is a member of the Ficidae, which are often referred to as the Fig Shells. It is a small family with only one genus. This species lives on sand in deep water.

| Common name: | Pacific Partridge Tun |
|---|---|
| Scientific name: | *Tonna perdix* |
| Descriptor: | Linnaeus, 1758 |
| Superfamily: | Tonnacea |
| Family: | Tonnidae |
| Distribution: | Indo-Pacific |
| Size: | 8in (200mm) |

The Pacific Partridge Tun is one of about 40 species in this family of large deep water mollusks. They only occur in tropical and warm temperate waters, where they live in sandy areas. They are thought to be carnivorous, and it is most likely that they feed on crabs, fish or sea-urchins, probably digested using strong secretions.

| | |
|---|---|
| **Common name:** | Geography Cone |
| **Scientific name:** | *Conus geographus* |
| **Descriptor:** | Linnaeus, 1758 |
| **Superfamily:** | Conacea |
| **Family:** | Conidae |
| **Distribution:** | Indo-Pacific |
| **Size:** | 5in (125mm) |

The cone family — the "Conidae" — is very extensive, with over 500 species of highly colored and often very varied shells. Some of them are very dangerous to handle when living, with some, notably the Geography and Textile cones, particularly lethal — they have been recorded as causing many human deaths. This is due to the fact that they are active hunters, and use powerful poisons via a sort of harpoon arrangement to subdue their prey, which is usually either worms, mollusks, or small fish. The cones are more or less restricted to the tropics, with only a few exceptions. They also form distinct races within certain areas. Some start life by going through a larval stage which is planktonic, whereas others hatch directly as small snails complete with miniature shells. They are often very popular with collectors, even though their identification can be a real problem, especially with species such as the Magus Cone. The Geography Cone is a common species, which all bathers and divers of the tropics should bear in mind. It lives on sandy bottoms amongst coral down to depths of about 30ft (9m).

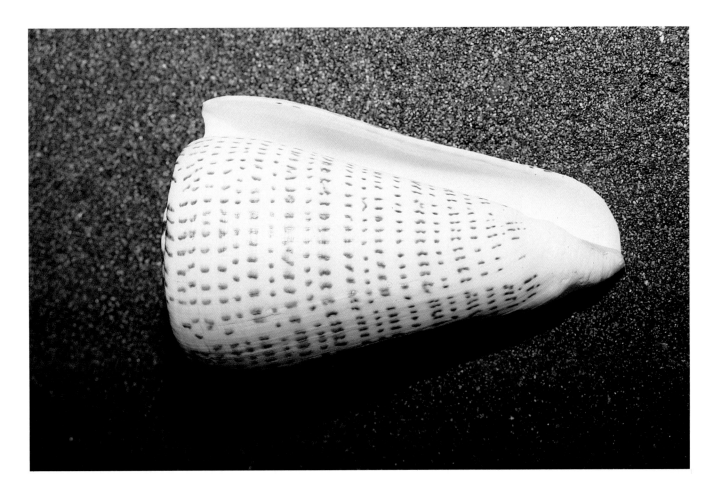

| Common name: | Leopard Cone |
|---|---|
| Scientific name: | *Conus leopardus* |
| Descriptor: | Roding, 1798 |
| Superfamily: | Conacea |
| Family: | Conidae |
| Distribution: | Indo-Pacific |
| Size: | 8.5in (220mm) |

The Leopard Cone is one of the largest cones, which coupled with its substantial construction also makes it one of the heaviest. It lives amongst sand near coral reefs of the Indian and Pacific Oceans, where it is a predator on many things, but mostly marine worms.

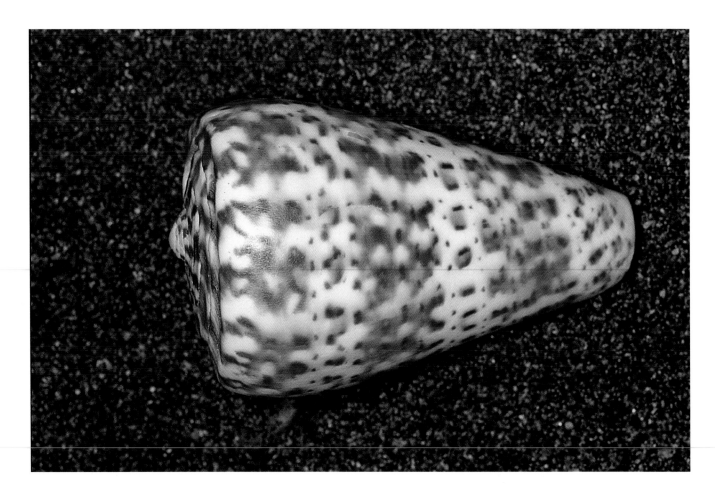

| | |
|---|---|
| **Common name:** | Butterfly Cone |
| **Scientific name:** | *Conus pulcher* |
| **Descriptor:** | Lightfoot, 1786 |
| **Superfamily:** | Conacea |
| **Family:** | Conidae |
| **Distribution:** | West Africa |
| **Size:** | 12 inches (300mm) |

The Butterfly Cone is the largest of its family, and is not a rare species, but it is uncommonly seen in collections. It is found along the coasts of central West Africa — the specimen illustrated here came from the Gambia.

| Common name: | Textile Cone |
|---|---|
| Scientific name: | *Conus textile* |
| Descriptor: | Linnaeus, 1758 |
| Superfamily: | Conacea |
| Family: | Conidae |
| Distribution: | Indo-Pacific |
| Size: | 3-4in (75-100mm) |

The Textile Cone is notorious for being one of the most dangerous of all mollusks. Its poison has caused several fatalities. As with the Geography Cone, it is particularly dangerous because it is common, and inhabits the very places that divers like to frequent — sandy places near coral reefs. They sometimes put their lives in danger by handling these lethal cones without realizing just how deadly they can be.

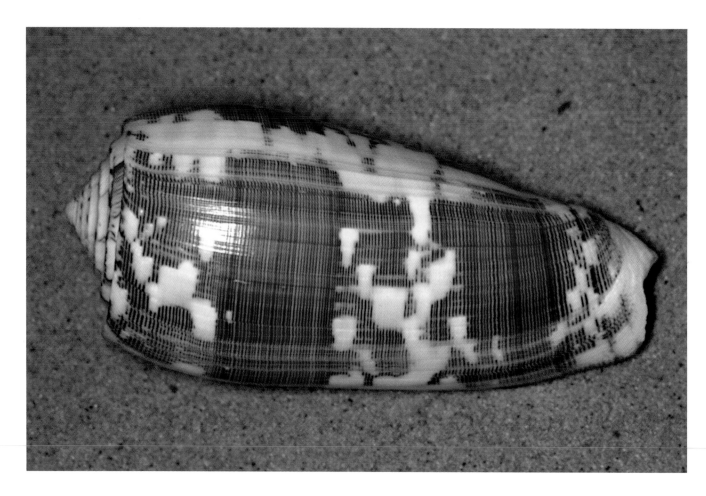

| Common name: | Striated Cone |
|---|---|
| Scientific name: | *Conus striatus* |
| Descriptor: | Linnaeus, 1758 |
| Superfamily: | Conacea |
| Family: | Conidae |
| Distribution: | Indo-Pacific |
| Size: | 3-6in (75-150mm) |

This is yet another common poisonous cone which lives on sandy bottoms amongst coral reefs. It is distributed throughout the tropical regions of the Indian and Pacific Oceans. It is quite variable in size and markings.

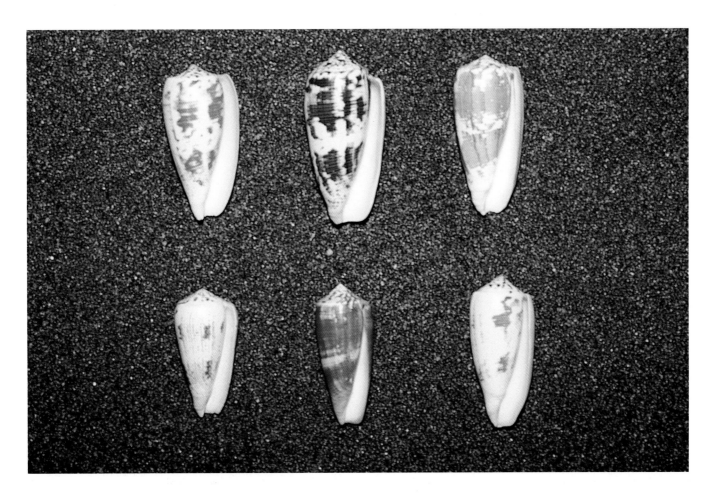

| Common name: | Magus Cone |
|---|---|
| Scientific name: | *Conus magus* |
| Descriptor: | Linnaeus, 1758 |
| Superfamily: | Conacea |
| Family: | Conidae |
| Distribution: | Indo-Pacific, Angola, Senegal |
| Size: | 3.25in (80mm) |

The Magus Cone is an excellent example of the collector's nightmare — it is so variable that it is very hard indeed to make a categorical identification. The group of six specimens shown here illustrate just how much they can vary. They occur across the Indian and Pacific Oceans, and also up the southwestern coasts of Africa.

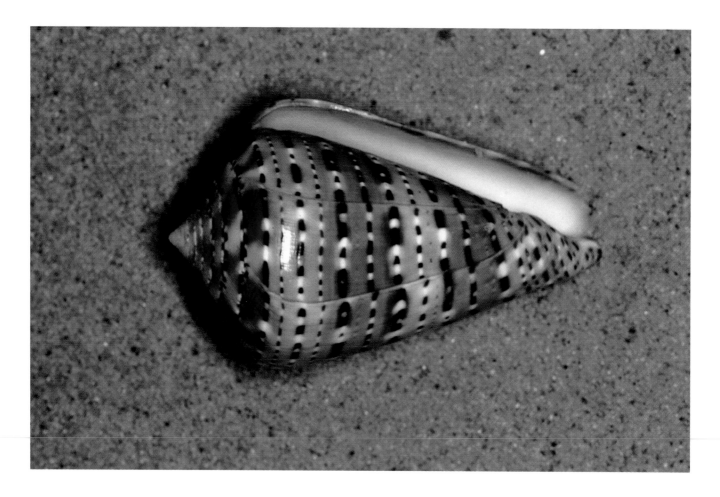

| | |
|---|---|
| **Common name:** | Genuanus Cone |
| **Scientific name:** | *Conus genuanus* |
| **Descriptor:** | Linnaeus, 1758 |
| **Superfamily:** | Conacea |
| **Family:** | Conidae |
| **Distribution:** | West Africa |
| **Size:** | 2-3in (50-75mm) |

The Genuanus Cone has a combination of markings and coloration that makes it a welcome addition to any collection, although good specimens are hard to come by. It lives in shallow waters among the sandy areas of the coral reefs of west Africa.

| Common name: | Fig Cone |
|---|---|
| Scientific name: | *Conus figulinus* |
| Descriptor: | Linnaeus, 1758 |
| Superfamily: | Conacea |
| Family: | Conidae |
| Distribution: | Indo-Pacific |
| Size: | 3.25in (80mm) |

The Fig Cone inhabits much the same environments as the Genuanus Cone, except that it lives in the Indian and Pacific Oceans instead of on the west coast of Africa. It can be found down to depths of about 60ft (18m), where it is common throughout its range.

| | |
|---|---|
| **Common name:** | Japanese Wonder Shell |
| **Scientific name:** | *Thatcheria mirabilis* |
| **Descriptor:** | Angas, 1877 |
| **Superfamily:** | Conacea |
| **Family:** | Turridae |
| **Distribution:** | Japan and Western Pacific Ocean |
| **Size:** | 3-4in (75-100mm) |

The Japanese Wonder Shell is one of about 1,200 species of "Turrids," which inhabit most of the waters around Japan and much of the western Pacific Ocean. The various members of this family are very variable in size, with this one being the largest. As this unmistakable shell is a member of the cones' superfamily; it uses a poisoned harpoon to hunt and kill its prey.

| Common name: | Marlinspike |
|---|---|
| Scientific name: | *Terebra maculata* |
| Descriptor: | Linnaeus, 1758 |
| Superfamily: | Conacea |
| Family: | Terebridae |
| Distribution: | Indo-Pacific |
| Size: | 10in (250mm) |

The Marlinspike is one of about 150 species of Auger shells, so called because an auger is a spiral drill shape. It is the largest species in the genus, and lives in the sandy bottoms of tropical and semi-tropical seas in the Indian and Pacific Oceans, where it is a predator on various marine creatures.

| | |
|---|---|
| **Common name:** | Judas Ear Shell or Midas Ear Cassidula |
| **Scientific name:** | *Ellobium aurismidae* |
| **Descriptor:** | Linnaeus, 1758 |
| **Superfamily:** | Melampiacea |
| **Family:** | Melampidae |
| **Distribution:** | Southwest Pacific |
| **Size:** | 2in (50mm) |

This shell goes under two very different common names, which are the "Judas Ear Shell" or the "Midas Ear Cassidula." It is unusual in that it is an air breather — that is, it cannot assimilate oxygen in the same way that most other marine mollusks can. It therefore lives in the shallows where it can come to the surface regularly.

| Common name: | Thick Keyhole Limpet |
|---|---|
| Scientific name: | *Fissurella crassa* |
| Descriptor: | Lamarck, 1822 |
| Superfamily: | Fissurellacea |
| Family: | Fissurellidae |
| Distribution: | West, central and south America |
| Size: | 1.5in (40mm) |

The Thick Keyhole Limpet is typical of the members of this family in that it has a hole in the "dorsum," which is the top of the shell. This is sometimes keyhole-shaped, hence the common name for the family. The various species of Keyhole Limpets are mostly found in areas of warm water, where they cling to rocks and coral and graze on plant matter.

| Common name: | Telescope Snail |
|---|---|
| Scientific name: | *Telescopium telescopium* |
| Descriptor: | Linnaeus, 1758 |
| Superfamily: | Cerithiacea |
| Family: | Potamididae |
| Distribution: | Indo-Pacific |
| Size: | 4in (100mm) |

The Telescope Snail lives in muddy habitats such as mangrove swamps and estuaries, where they live an herbivorous existence, feeding off algae and other plant material. Both their common and scientific names are indicative of their similarity to a telescopic structure. In some areas, native tribes used them to make small trumpets.

| | |
|---|---|
| **Common name:** | Lined Moon |
| **Scientific name:** | *Natica lineata* |
| **Descriptor:** | Roding, 1798 |
| **Superfamily:** | Naticacea |
| **Family:** | Naticidae |
| **Distribution:** | Japan, northern Australia, northern Indian Ocean |
| **Size:** | 1.5in (40mm) |

The Lined Moon is one of a family that is often referred to as either "Moon Snails" or "Necklace Shells," of which there are over a hundred species. This one, like most others lives around sandy beaches in tropical areas.

| | |
|---|---|
| **Common name:** | Ruddy Frog Shell |
| **Scientific name:** | *Bursa rubeta* |
| **Descriptor:** | Linnaeus, 1758 |
| **Superfamily:** | Cymatiacea |
| **Family:** | Bursidae |
| **Distribution:** | Indo-Pacific |
| **Size:** | 10in (250mm) |

The Ruddy Frog is a typical "Frog Shell", being a large and heavily built species. They were once collected for use as oil lamps from rocky areas and coral reefs throughout the Indian and Pacific Oceans.

| | |
|---|---|
| **Common name:** | Black-Spotted Triton |
| **Scientific name:** | *Cymatium lotorium* |
| **Descriptor:** | Linnaeus, 1758 |
| **Superfamily:** | Cymatiacea |
| **Family:** | Cymatiidae |
| **Distribution:** | Indian, Pacific, and Japonic areas |
| **Size:** | 4-6.25in (100-160mm) |

The Black-Spotted Triton has a heavily built solid shell that in the past made it popular with native tribes for a variety of uses. The living mollusk is carnivorous, preying on many different marine creatures.

| | |
|---|---|
| **Common name:** | Panama Horse Conch |
| **Scientific name:** | *Pleuroploca princeps* |
| **Descriptor:** | Genus, Fischer, 1884 |
| **Superfamily:** | Cymatiacea |
| **Family:** | Fasciolariidae |
| **Genus:** | Pleuroploca |
| **Distribution:** | Central America |
| **Size:** | 10in (250mm) |

The Panama Horse Conch is one of several large species that are known as "Horse Conchs" or "Tulip" shells. The biggest can grow to about 20in (500mm), but this species is smaller than that. They are predatory mollusks, mostly on other shell species, especially those in the clam families.

| Common name: | Fox's Head |
|---|---|
| Scientific name: | *Fasciolaria trapezium* |
| Descriptor: | Linnaeus, 1758 |
| Superfamily: | Cymatiacea |
| Family: | Fasciolariidae |
| Genus: | Pleuroploca |
| Distribution: | Indo-Pacific |
| Size: | 8in (200mm) |

The Fox's Head is another member of the tulip shell family, and like the others, it has a solid, heavy shell. Its common name is due to the fact that, when it is held at a certain angle, it looks like a fox's head!

# Reference

## Shell Magazines

There are several magazines and journals devoted to the study of mollusks, either as shells or as living organisms. I have listed some of them here — they range from scientific publications for learned academics, through to those for shell collectors. Some specialist magazines will send sample copies before you subscribe to them, so it is worth contacting them if you would like to "see before you buy."

*The Veliger* (ISSN 0042-3211)
This is an international, scientific quarterly published by the California Malacozoological Society.

*Vita Marina*
This quarterly publication is a high quality journal on shells, which reviews species from various parts of the world, including their families, their biology, and so on.

*La Conchiglia*
This is another quarterly publication on shells. It is in full-color, with information about many subjects to do with shells, including reviews, descriptions of new species, collecting trips, and background information.

**Below: The Ruddy Frog Shell; see page 122.**

*Of Sea and Shore*
This magazine is yet another which is published quarterly. It contains features on collecting shells in exotic places, articles on shells, and others on shells of marine and freshwater environments, including — as the title suggests — those from the shores of these habitats. It also has regular columns covering shells on stamps, book reviews, exchange offers, club news, regulations on collecting, ads from shell dealers from around the world, and more.

## Shell Related Internet Sites

There are huge numbers of web-sites on the internet concerning shells of one sort or another. If you are new to "surfing the web," call up a "search" page, and enter "shells," "mollusks", or "malacology" as your search keywords. You will then be presented with lots of sites from which to choose. When you find one that interests you, you can either read it immediately, or you can save it in a file, and then read it later. This is the best thing to do if you are paying for your telephone calls, or if you pay for your internet access by the hour. If you want to access some sites directly, you can try the ones listed below. I hope they are still extant by the time you read this — nothing is ever stable in the world of computers!

This is a site devoted to European Malacological Societies:
http://www.aicon.com/sim/europe/

The "Conchologists of America Information Centre":
http://coa.acnatsci.org/conchnet/

This is a site about the Giant Squid:
http://seawifs.gsfc.nasa.gov/squid.html

This is a page devoted to Cephalopods:
http://is.dal.ca/~ceph/wood.html

A gallery of mainly land and freshwater snails from Singapore and Malaysia:
http://home1.pacific.net.sg/~chansy/

An illustrated guide to the diverse freshwater snails of Florida:
http://www.flmnh.ufl.edu/natsci/malacology/fl-snail/snails1.htm

An extensive list of mollusk links:
http://www.york.biosis.org/zrdocs/zoolinfo/grp_moll.htm

All you want to know about mollusks and malacologists worldwide:
http://fly.hiwaay.net/~dwills/shellnet.html

# Books On Shells — References & Bibliography

Abbott, R. Tucker; *Shells*; National Audobon Society, Doubleday, 1966.
Abbott, R. Tucker & Zim, H. S.; *Seashells of the World*; Hamlyn, 1967
Abbott, R. Tucker; *Kingdom of the Seashell*; Hamlyn, 1973.
Angel, H.; *Seashore Life on Sandy Beaches*; Jarrold, 1975.
Angel, H.. *Sea Shells of the Seashore, Book 2*; Jarrold, 1976, 1978.
Angel, H.; *Sea Shells of the Seashore, Book 1*; Jarrold, 1978.
Barrett, J. & Yonge, C. M.; *Pocket Guide to the Sea Shore*; Collins, 1973.
Beer, T.; *Devon's Fossils, Pebbles & Shells*; Pike, 1974.
Brind, R.; *Common Sea Shells*; Exeter Museum. c1980.
Cameron, R.; *Shells, Pleasures and Treasures*; Weidenfeld & Nicolson, 1961.

All the photographs in this book were supplied by Simon Coombes of True Colours except for the following: pp2, 7, 9, 12, 13, 17, 26, 27, 28, 29, 30, 31, 30, 31, 41, 42, 43, 44, 45, 46, 47, 50, 51, 127 (Pictor International, London); and 14, 22 (Author's Collection).

Cameron, R.; *Shells, Pleasures and Treasures*; Octopus, 1972.

Christensen, J. M. & Dance, S. P.; *Seashells — Bivalves*; Penguin Nature, 1980.

Clarke, Arthur H.; *The Freshwater Molluscs of Canada*; National Museum of Natural Sciences, Ottawa, 1981.

Clayton, J. M.; *Seashells*; Octopus, 1974.

Cox, I. (ed.); *The Scallop*; Shell, 1957.

Cummings, K. S.; *Guide to Freshwater Mussels of the Midwest*; Illinois, 1992.

Dance, S. P..; *Shell Collecting*; Faber, 1966.

Dance, S. P.; *Shells and Shell Collecting*; Hamlyn, 1972.

Dance, S. P.; *Seashells*; Hamlyn, 1974.

Duncan, F. M.; *British Shells*; King Penguin, 1943.

French, G. & Freeman, D.; *What Sea Shell Is That?*; Purnell, 1969.

Habe, T; *Shells of Japan*; Hoikusha, 1971.

Harasewych, M. G.; *Shells — Jewels from the Sea*; Courage, 1991.

Hinton, A.; *Shells of New Guinea & the Central Indo-Pacific*; Robert Brown, 1972.

Hodgson, M. K.; The Spell of the Shell; Deutsch, 1976.

Kearney M. P. and Cameron, R. A. D.; *A field guide of the land snails of Britain and North-west Europe*;Wm. Collings & Sons, Glasgow, 1979.

Lindbergh, A. M.; *Gift From The Sea*; Pantheon, 1955.

Mondadori, A.; *The Macdonald Encyclopedia of Shells*; 1982.

Morris, P. A.; *Shells Of The Atlantic & Gulf Coasts & W. Indies*; Houghton, 1973.

Morton, J. E.; *Molluscs*; Hutchinson, 1958.

Murray, S. B.; *Seashell Identifier*; Sterling. c1975.

Oliver, A. P. H.; *Shells of the World*; Hamlyn.

Price, A. F.; *An Introduction to Tropical Sea Shells*; c. 1960.

Rimmer, R.; *The Land & Freshwater Shells of the British Isles*; Grant, 1880.

Rogers, J. E.; *The Shell Book*; C. T. Branford, 1951.

Senders, J. & R.; *Shells, A Collectors Guide*; David & Charles, 1984.

Sharabati, D.; *Saudi Arabian Seashells*; VNU, 1981.

Smyth, J. C.; *Shells and Shellfish*; Oliver & Boyd, 1968.

Sowerby, G. B.; *Thesaurus Conchyliorum, Vol. I*; 1981, reprint of 1847.

Spry, J. F.; *The Sea Shells of Dar es Salaam, Part I*; 1964 and 1968 2nd rev. ed.

Step, E.; *Shell Life, An Introduction to the British Mollusca*; Warne, W & W, 1960.

Stix, H. & M., & Abbott, R. Tucker; *The Shell, 500M yrs of Inspired Des.*; Abrams.

Wagner, R. & Abbott, R. Tucker; *Van Nostrand's Standard Catalogue of Shells*; 1967.

Wilson, B. R.; *Australian Shells*; Reed, rev. ed, 1980.

Woodward, S. P.; *A Manual of the Mollusca*; Lockwood, 1875.

Young, G.; *By The Sea*; Jarrold, 1981.